# Garden Plants
## *for*
# Kansas

*Annie Calovich • Laura Peters*

Lone Pine Publishing International

**The Distributor: Lone Pine Publishing**
1808 B Street NW, Suite 140
Auburn, WA, USA 98001
Website: www.lonepinepublishing.com.

**Library and Archives Canada Cataloguing in Publication**

Calovich, Annie
Best garden plants for Kansas / Annie Calovich, Laura Peters.

Includes index.
ISBN 978-976-8200-32-7

1. Plants, Ornamental--Kansas. 2. Gardening--Kansas.
I. Peters, Laura, 1968- II. Title.

SB453.2.K2C34 2007    635.09781   C2006-905471-1

Front cover photographs *(clockwise from top right)*: lily *(Erika Flatt)*, Sunsprite rose, iris, daylily, lilac *(Tamara Eder)*, daylily *(Alison Penko)*, lily *(Laura Peters)*, coreopsis *(Tim Matheson)*, *(center)* crabapple *(Tim Matheson)*.

All photos by Tim Matheson, Tamara Eder and Laura Peters except:
Agriculture and Agri-Food Canada (Morden Research Station) 127b; Bailey Nursery Roses 117b; Doris Baucom 30a; Sandra Bit 89a; Brenden Casement 83b; Conard-Pyle Roses 125a; Dan Turner-Elko Roses 124a; Janet Davis 127a; Joan de Gray 52a; Don Doucette 103b, 113b; Jen Fafard 143a; Derek Fell 29a, 29b, 51a, 79a, 79b, 95a, 95b, 96a, 96b, 109b, 130b, 136b, 137; Erika Flatt 141b, 145a; Gene Sasse-Weeks Roses 125b; Anne Gordon 87a, 87b; Saxon Holt 60a, 116, 117a; Duncan Kelbaugh 141a; Liz Klose 60b; Debra Knapke 59a, 132a; Dawn Loewen 69a, 75b, 81a, 81b; Janet Loughrey 124b; Marilynn McAra 143b, 144b; Steve Nikkila 59b; Kim O'Leary 12b, 13a, 21a, 21b, 40a, 128b, 140a; Allison Penko 10, 46a, 54a, 63a, 75a, 77b, 83a, 97a, 104a, 107a, 107b, 108a, 110a, 129b, 131a, 140b, 157a, 162, 165b; Photos.com 61a, 144a 146a; Robert Ritchie 39b, 42a, 44a, 56a, 56b, 71a, 72a, 72b, 82a, 82b, 102a, 110b, 126a, 151a; Leila Sidi 146b; Peter Thompstone 17b, 18a, 49a, 163b; Mark Turner 91b, 136a; Don Williamson 139b, 142a, 142b, 148a; Tim Wood 71b, 78a, 105a, 109a, 112a, 113a, 114a, 134a.

PC: *P13*

# Table of Contents

Introduction. . . . . . . . . . . . . . . . . . . . . . . . . . . . . . 4

Annuals . . . . . . . . . . . . . . . . . . . . . . . . . . . . . . . 11

Perennials . . . . . . . . . . . . . . . . . . . . . . . . . . . . . 37

Trees & Shrubs. . . . . . . . . . . . . . . . . . . . . . . . . . 69

Roses . . . . . . . . . . . . . . . . . . . . . . . . . . . . . . . 115

Vines . . . . . . . . . . . . . . . . . . . . . . . . . . . . . . . 127

Bulbs . . . . . . . . . . . . . . . . . . . . . . . . . . . . . . . 137

Herbs . . . . . . . . . . . . . . . . . . . . . . . . . . . . . . . 147

Ferns, Grasses & Groundcovers . . . . . . . . . . . 157

Glossary . . . . . . . . . . . . . . . . . . . . . . . . . . . . . 171
Index . . . . . . . . . . . . . . . . . . . . . . . . . . . . . . . 172
About the Authors/Acknowledgments . . . . . . 176

# Introduction

Starting a garden can seem like a daunting task, but it's also an exciting and rewarding adventure. With so many plants to choose from, the challenge is to decide which ones will work best here in Kansas. This book is intended to give beginning gardeners the information they need to start planning and planting gardens of their own. It includes a wide variety of plants and provides basic plant descriptions, planting and growing information and tips for use. With this book at hand, you can begin to produce a beautiful and functional landscape in your own yard.

The "Sunflower State" experiences a wide range of temperatures throughout the year given its distance from the moderating influences of the ocean. It is here, in the middle of the country, where woodlands fade to prairie, the humid East starts to give way to the dry West and the northern turf region of cool-season grasses transitions to the southern region of warm-season grasses.

Precipitation is also variable throughout the state. Rainfall averages increase from approximately 15" in the western portion of the state to 45" in the southeast, an average increase of about 1" every 18 miles from west to east. The vast majority of the annual precipitation falls between April and September, but the summer heat often causes the evaporation rates to increase substantially, resulting in a dry season. Western Kansas experiences the highest levels of precipitation variability and often the lowest average rainfall totals.

The winters are cold but relatively mild throughout the state. Snow is always beneficial with the water it provides, and its insulative value against the cold helps winter annuals and perennials make it through the colder days of winter. The northern portion of Kansas receives the largest volume of snow throughout the winter and it remains on the ground for longer periods compared to warmer zones.

The average length of the growing season, from the last killing frost in spring to the first killing frost in the fall, ranges from approximately 160 days in length in the northwest to 195 days in south-central and southeastern Kansas. Kansas is also fortunate to have long summer daylight hours. Days in late June are approximately one hour longer in Kansas compared to Florida or southern Texas. A combination of warmer zones and a lengthy growing season offers a wealth of gardening opportunities throughout the state.

With such variability in climate conditions comes the choices of what to plant and where to plant, along with an opportunity to experiment with your own garden, and what's more fun than trying new things from one year to another?

## Climate

Hardiness zones and frost dates are two terms often used when discussing climate and gardening. Hardiness zones are based on the minimum possible winter temperatures, and plants are rated according to the zones in which they grow successfully. The last frost date in spring combined with the first frost date in fall allows us to predict the length of the growing season and gives us an idea of when we can begin planting.

Microclimates are small areas that are generally warmer or colder than the surrounding area. Buildings, fences, trees and other large structures can provide extra shelter in winter but may trap heat in summer, thus creating a warmer microclimate. The bottoms of hills are usually colder than the tops but may not be as windy. Take advantage of these areas when you plan your garden and choose your plants; you may even grow out-of-zone plants successfully in a warm, sheltered location.

## Getting Started

When planning your garden, start with a quick analysis of the garden as it is now. Plants have different requirements and it is best to put the right plant in the right place rather than to try to change your garden to suit the plants you want.

Knowing which parts of your garden receive the most and least amounts of sunlight will help you choose the proper plants and decide where to plant them. Light is classified into four basic groups: full sun (direct, unobstructed light all or most of the day); partial shade (direct sun for about half the day and shade for the rest); light shade (shade all or most of the day with some sun filtering through to ground level); and full shade (no direct sunlight). Most plants prefer a specific amount of light, but many can adapt to a range of light levels.

The soil is the foundation of a good garden. Plants use the soil to hold themselves upright and rely on the many resources it contains: air, water, nutrients, organic matter and a host of microbes. The soil

## Hardiness Zones Map

Average Annual Minimum Temperature

-15 to -20
-10 to -15
-5 to -10
0 to -5

Kansas City
Topeka
Lawrence

Wichita

particle size influences the amount of air, water and nutrients the soil can hold. Sand, with the largest particles, has a lot of air space and allows water and nutrients to drain quickly. Clay, with the smallest particles, is high in nutrients but has very little air space; water is, therefore, slow to penetrate clay and slow to drain from it.

Soil acidity or alkalinity (measured on the pH scale) influences the amount and type of nutrients available to plants. A pH of 7 is neutral; a lower pH is more acidic. Most plants prefer a soil with a pH of 5.5–7.5. Soil-testing kits are available at most garden centers, and soil samples can be sent to testing labs for a more thorough analysis of pH and nutrients in the soil. They will give you an idea of which plants will do well in your soil and what amendments your soil might need.

Compost is one of the best and most important amendments you can add to any type of soil. Compost improves soil by adding organic matter and nutrients, introducing soil microbes, increasing water retention and improving drainage. You can purchase compost or you can make it in your own backyard.

## Selecting Plants

It's important to purchase healthy plants that are free of pests and disease. Such plants will establish quickly in your garden and will not introduce problems that may spread to other plants. You should have a good idea of what the plant is supposed to look like—its habit and the color and shape of its leaves—and then inspect the plant for signs of disease or insect damage before buying it.

The majority of plants are grown in containers or nursery pots. This way is efficient for nurseries and greenhouses to grow plants, but when plants grow in a restricted space for too long, they can become pot bound with their roots densely encircling the inside of the pot. Avoid purchasing plants in this condition; they are often stressed and can take longer to establish. It is often possible to remove the pot temporarily to look at the condition of the plant roots. You can check for soil-borne insects, rotten roots and girdling or pot-bound roots at the same time. Roots that are wrapped densely around the inside of a pot must be lightly pruned or teased apart before planting.

## Planting Basics

The following tips apply to all plants.
• Prepare the garden before planting. Remove weeds, make any needed amendments and dig or till the soil in preparation for planting if you are starting a new landscape. The prepared area should be the size of the plant's mature root system.
• Settle the soil with water. Good contact between the roots and the soil is important, but if you press the soil down too

Gently remove container.

Ensure proper planting depth.

Backfill with soil.

firmly, as often happens when you step on it, you can cause compaction. This reduces the movement of water through the soil and leaves very few air spaces. Instead, pour water in as you fill the hole with soil. The water will settle the soil evenly without allowing it to compact.

• If the soil is heavy and clumpy after a spring snowstorm or rainfall, wait until it dries out and becomes crumbly again before working it.

• Unwrap the roots. It is always best to remove any container to give the roots the chance to spread out naturally when planted. If the rootball is firm enough and will remain solid without support, the container can be removed before the plant is placed into the planting hole. If the rootball is not solid, the container should only be removed after the plant is properly placed and is and supported by surrounding soil; otherwise, during transplanting, soil will fall away bringing with it some of the tender feeder roots.

In particular, you should remove plastic containers, fiber pots, wire and burlap when planting trees. Fiber pots decompose very slowly, if at all, and they wick moisture away from the plant. Synthetic burlap won't decompose, and wire will eventually girdle or strangle the roots as they mature. The peat pots and pellets used to start annuals decompose more readily and can be planted with the young transplants. Even these peat pots should be sliced down the sides, and any part of the pot that will be exposed above ground should be removed to prevent water from being wicked away from the roots.

• Accommodate the rootball. The general rule of thumb for the size of the planting hole is at least two times the width of the rootball but no deeper than its height. If the rootball is planted too deeply, the plant will have a difficult time and may even die. The top surface of the rootball should be either level with the surrounding soil or a fraction of an inch below the surrounding soil level but no deeper. Tender roses are the only exception to this rule.

• Know the mature size of your plants. You should space your plants based on how big the plants will be when they are mature, rather than how big they are when you plant them. For example, a shrub that will grow to be 10' tall and wide may only be 12" when you buy and plant it. Large plants should have enough room to mature without interfering with walls, roof overhangs, power lines, walkways and surrounding plants.

• Identify your plants. Keep track of what's what in your garden by putting a tag next to each plant when you plant it. A gardening journal is also a great place to list the plants you have and where you planted them. It is very easy, for beginning and seasoned gardeners alike, to forget exactly what they planted and where they planted it.

Settle backfilled soil with water.

Water the plant well.

Add a layer of mulch.

• Water deeply. It's better to water deeply when necessary than to water lightly more often. Deep and thorough watering forces roots to grow as they search for water and helps them survive dry spells. Always check the rootzone before you water as some soils hold more water for longer periods than other soils. Mulching helps retain moisture and reduces watering needs. Containers and container gardens, are the watering exception as they can quickly dry out and may even need watering every day, in fact often more than once. The best way to determine if it's time to water is by poking your finger into the top inch or so of the soil or potting mix. If it's dry more than an inch under the surface, it's time to water.

### Choosing Plants

When choosing your plants, try to aim for a variety of sizes, shapes, textures, features and bloom times. Features, such as decorative fruit, variegated or colorful leaves and interesting bark, provide interest when plants aren't blooming. This way you will have a garden that captivates your attention all year.

### Annuals

Annuals are planted new each year and are only expected to last for a single growing season. Their flowers and decorative foliage provide bright splashes of color and can fill in spaces around immature trees, shrubs and perennials.

Annuals are easy to plant and are often sold in small cell-packs of four or six plants. The roots quickly fill the space in these small packs, so the small rootball should be broken up before planting. Split the ball in two up the center or run your thumb up each side to break up the roots.

Many annuals are grown from seed and can be started directly in the garden once the soil has begun to warm up.

### Perennials

Perennials grow for three or more years. They usually die back to the ground each fall and send up new shoots in spring, though they can also be evergreen or semi-shrubby. They often have a shorter period of bloom than annuals but require less care.

Many perennials benefit from being divided every few years, usually in early spring while plants are still dormant or, with some plants, after flowering. Dividing keeps them growing and blooming vigorously, and in some cases controls their spread. It involves digging the plant up, removing dead debris, breaking the plant into several pieces using a sharp knife, spade or saw and replanting some or all of the pieces. Extra bits can be shared with family, friends and neighbors.

### Trees & Shrubs

Trees and shrubs provide the bones of the garden. They are often the slowest growing plants but usually live the longest. Characterized by leaf type, they may be deciduous or evergreen, and needled or broad-leaved. Choose a diversity of trees for a healthy and interesting landscape.

Trees should have as little disturbed soil as possible at the bottom of the planting hole. Loose dirt settles over

Annuals provide color and flexibility in the garden.

time, and sinking even 1" can kill some trees. The prepared area for trees and shrubs needs to be at least two to four times wider than the rootball.

Staking, sometimes recommended for newly planted trees, is only necessary for trees over 5' tall. Stakes support the rootball until it grows enough to support the tree. Stakes should be placed at a southwest angle and make sure to use ties that won't cut into the bark. Stakes should allow the trunk to move with the wind and should only remain in place for one year or less.

Pruning is required more often for shrubs than trees and even then, only to remove dead or diseased wood. A woody plant is often pruned to control its growth when it is planted in a location that won't allow for its mature size. Pruning should never be used for this reason, and this situation can be avoided by researching what tree and shrub is best for a location based on space and light, etc. Pruning can be a benefit to fruiting trees however, as well as some flowering trees and shrubs.

### Roses

Roses are beautiful shrubs with lovely, often-fragrant blooms. Traditionally, most roses only bloomed once in the growing season, but new varieties bloom all, or almost all, summer. Repeat-blooming, or recurrent, roses should be deadheaded to encourage more flower production. One-time bloomers should be left in place for the colorful hips that develop.

Generally, roses prefer a fertile, well-prepared planting area. A rule of thumb is to prepare an area at least twice the width of the rootball or a minimum of 24" in width for bareroot roses. Add plenty of compost or other fertile organic matter, and keep the roots well watered during the growing season. Many roses are quite durable and will

Training vines to climb arbors adds structure to the garden.

adapt to poorer conditions. Grafted roses should be planted with the graft right at the soil line. When watering, avoid getting water on the foliage to reduce the spread of blackspot. Clean up any leaves infected with blackspot from the plant and the ground to keep the disease from spreading.

Roses, like all plants, have specific pruning requirements. Consult with your local extension department or garden center for specific information pertaining to pruning your roses.

### Vines

Vines or climbing plants add depth to the garden and are useful for screening and shade, especially in a location too small for a tree. They may be woody or herbaceous and annual or perennial. Vines may cling to surfaces, may have wrapping tendrils or stems or may need to be tied in place with string.

Sturdy trellises, arbors, porch railings, fences, obelisks, pergolas, walls, poles and trees are all possible vine supports. If a support is needed, ensure it's in place before you plant the vine to avoid disturbing the roots later. Choose a support that is suitable for the vine you are growing. The support needs to be sturdy enough to hold the plant up and should match the growing habit of the vine—whether clinging, wrapping or tied.

### Bulbs, Corms & Tubers

These plants have fleshy, underground storage organs that allow them to survive extended periods of dormancy. They are often grown for the bright splashes of color their flowers provide. They may be spring, summer or fall flowering. Each has an ideal depth and time of year at which it should be planted.

Hardy bulbs can be left in the ground and will flower every year. Some popular, tender plants are grown from bulbs, corms or tubers and are generally lifted or removed from the soil in late summer or fall as the foliage dies back. These are stored in a cool, frost-free location for winter, to be replanted in spring.

### Herbs

Herbs are plants with medicinal, culinary or other economic purposes. A few common culinary herbs are included in this book. Even if you don't cook with herbs, the often-fragrant foliage adds its aroma to the garden, and the plants can be quite decorative in form, leaf and flower. A conveniently placed container of your favorite herbs—perhaps located near the kitchen door—will yield plenty of flavor and fragrance all summer.

Ornamental grasses add color, variety and texture.

Many herbs have pollen-producing flowers that attract butterflies, bees, hummingbirds and beneficial insects to your garden. Beneficial insects feast on problem insects, such as aphids, mealybugs and whiteflies.

### Ferns, Grasses & Groundcovers

Many plants are grown for their decorative foliage rather than their flowers. Ornamental grasses, ferns, groundcovers and other foliage plants add a variety of colors, textures and forms to the garden. Many of these are included in other sections of this book, but we have set aside a few for the unique touch their foliage, form and habit adds to the garden.

Ferns provide a lacy foliage accent and combine attractively with broad-leaved perennials and shrubs. Ferns are common in moist, shady gardens but some selections will also thrive in the sunshine.

Ornamental grasses and grass-like plants provide interest throughout the year, even in the winter when the withered blades and seedheads are left to add motion and contrast to a brown landscape. They are cut back in early spring and divided when the clumps begin to die out in the centers.

Plants used for groundcovers are often vigorous, spreading or procumbent. These types of plants are frequently used as an alternative to grass, around the base of other, taller plants as a living mulch, to prevent erosion or purely for decorative purposes.

### A Final Comment

The more you discover about the fascinating world of plants—whether from reading, talking to other gardeners, appreciating the creative designs of others or experimenting with something new in your own garden—the more rewarding your gardening experience will become. Start gardening and let your passion for plants germinate and grow!

# Bacopa
### *Sutera*

Bacopa snuggles under and around the stems of taller plants, forming a dense carpet dotted with tiny, white to pale lavender flowers. It eventually grows over pot edges to form a waterfall of stars.

## Growing

Bacopa grows well in **partial shade**, with protection from the hot afternoon sun. The soil should be of **average fertility, humus rich, moist** and **well drained**.

Don't allow this plant to dry out or the leaves will quickly die. Cutting back dead growth may encourage new shoots to form.

## Tips

Bacopa is a popular plant for hanging baskets, mixed containers and window boxes. It is not recommended as a bedding plant because it fizzles quickly when the weather gets hot, particularly if you forget to water. Plant it where you'll see it every day so you'll remember to water it.

## Recommended

**S. cordata** is a compact, trailing plant that bears small white flowers all summer. Cultivars with larger white flowers, lavender flowers or gold and green variegated foliage are available.

*S. cordata* (above & below)

*Bacopa is a perennial that is grown as an annual outdoors. It will thrive as a houseplant in a bright room.*

**Features:** decorative flowers, foliage and habit; white or lavender flowers **Height:** 3–6" **Spread:** 12–20"

# Begonia
*Begonia*

*B. Rex Cultorum* hybrid 'Escargot' (above)
*B. semperflorens* (below)

With their beautiful flowers, compact habit and decorative foliage, begonias are sure to fulfill your shade-gardening needs.

## Growing
**Light to full shade** is best for this plant, though some wax begonias tolerate sun if their soil is kept moist. The soil should be **fertile, rich in organic matter** and **well drained** with a **neutral or acidic pH**. Allow the soil to dry out slightly between waterings, particularly for tuberous begonias.

Begonias love warm weather, so don't plant them out before the soil warms in spring. If they sit in cold soil, they may become stunted and fail to thrive.

## Tips
All begonias are useful for shaded garden beds and planters. The trailing, tuberous varieties can be used in hanging baskets and along rock walls, where the flowers will cascade over the edges.

Wax begonias have a neat, rounded habit that makes them particularly attractive as edging plants.

## Recommended
*B.* x *hybrida* Dragon Wing is a variety with deep scarlet to deep pink flowers and angel-winged foliage. This plant grows 12–15" tall and 15–18" wide, and it is heat tolerant.

*B. semperflorens* (wax begonias) have pink, white, red or bicolored flowers and green, bronze, reddish or white-variegated foliage. **Cocktail Series** is highly recommended for its reliability, color and habit.

*B.* x *tuberhybrida* (tuberous begonias) are popular for their large, cascading flowers that grow in many shades of red, pink, yellow, orange or white. **Non-Stop Series** is one of the more popular recommendations for Kansas.

**Features:** pink, white, red, yellow, orange, bicolored or picotee flowers; decorative foliage **Height:** 6–36" **Spread:** 6–24"

# Castor Bean

*Ricinus*

This vigorous annual can reach enormous heights in a relatively short span of time. Its exotic leaves and stature are ideally suited to large informal beds, and they make a great impact in containers.

## Growing

Castor bean requires a location in **full sun**. The soil should be **rich** and **loose** with **good drainage**.

## Tips

Castor bean suits background plantings and borders because it grows so quickly. It can obscure unsightly areas, such as garbage cans, air conditioners, utility boxes and meters, in a short period of time. Though this plant grows well in containers, a small container may stunt its overall growth.

Contact with castor bean's nicked or damaged seeds, spiny seedpods and leaves may cause an allergic reaction.

## Recommended

*R. communis* produces huge, deeply lobed, palm-like leaves and spiky, rounded seedpods. Interesting and colorful cultivars are available.

*R. communis* 'Sanguineus' (above)
*R. communis* (below)

*Castor bean requires little care and is very tolerant of hot and dry conditions.*

**Features:** large, ornate foliage; growth habit
**Height:** 8–10'  **Spread:** 5–7'

# Cockscomb

*Celosia*

C. argentea Plumosa Group (above)
C. argentea Cristata Group (below)

*To dry the colorful plumes, pick the flowers when they are at their peak and hang them upside down in a cool, shaded place. Collect the seeds that drop.*

If you've never grown cockscomb, give it a shot—you'll love the novelty of the Cristata's amazing flower head or the airy, feather-like flower spikes of the wheat celeosis.

### Growing

A sheltered spot in **full sun** is best. The soil should be **fertile, moist** and **well drained**, with plenty of **organic matter** worked in.

Cockscomb grow best when directly sown in the garden. If starting indoors, seed in peat pots or pellets and plant them before they begin to flower. Keep seeds moist and do not cover them.

### Tips

Plant cockscomb in borders, beds and planters. The flowers make interesting additions to fresh or dried arrangements. Crested varieties work well as accents and as cut flowers.

### Recommended

*C. argentea* is the parent of the many crested and plume-type varieties and cultivars now available. **Cristata Group** (crested celosia, cockscomb) has blooms that resemble brains or rooster combs. **Plumosa Group** (plume celosia) has plume-like blooms. Both groups have many varieties and cultivars.

*C. spicata* (*C. argentea* Spicata Group; wheat celosia) flowers often have a metallic sheen. **'Flamingo Feather'** has slender spikes of pink to white flowers. **'Flamingo Purple'** bears spikes of purple to white flowers and dark red-green stems and leaves.

**Features:** intensely colorful; interesting red, orange, gold, yellow, pink, purple flowers **Height:** 6"–4' **Spread:** equal to or slightly less than height

# Coleus
*Solenostemon (Coleus)*

From brash yellows, oranges and reds to deep maroon and rose selections, coleus colors, textures and variations are almost limitless.

## Growing
Coleus prefers to grow in **light** or **partial shade,** but tolerates full shade that isn't too dense. Selections known as sun coleus prefer full sun. The soil should be of **rich to average fertility, humus rich, moist** and **well drained.**

Place the seeds in a refrigerator for one or two days before planting them on the soil surface; the cold temperatures will help break the seeds' dormancy. They need light to germinate. Seedlings are green at first, but leaf variegation will develop as the plants mature. Coleus is also easy to propagate from 3" cuttings.

## Tips
The bold, colorful foliage is dramatic when coleus are grouped together as edging plants or in beds, borders or mixed containers. Coleus can also be grown indoors as a houseplant in a bright room.

Pinch off flower buds when they develop; the plants tend to stretch out and become less attractive after they flower.

## Recommended
*S. scutellarioides (Coleus blumei* var. *verschaffeltii)* forms a bushy mound of foliage. The leaf edges range from slightly toothed to very ruffled. Leaves are usually multi-colored with shades ranging from pale greenish yellow to deep purple-black. Sun-loving varieties

S. *scutellarioides* cultivars (above & below)

grown from cuttings include **'Alabama Sunset'** with spectacular orange, red and yellow leaves; **'Dark Star'** with dark, rich purple-black, scalloped leaves and **'Life Lime'** that bears large, gold leaves with occasional splashes of maroon. Many of the dozens of cultivars cannot be started from seed.

**Features:** brightly colored foliage; light purple flowers **Height:** 6–36" **Spread:** usually equal to height

# Cosmos

*Cosmos*

Cosmos flowers are deeply saturated with color and provide nectar for various butterflies. Their fluted petals add an interesting texture to the garden and the flower vase.

### Growing

Cosmos like **full sun**. The soil should be of **poor** or **average fertility** and **well drained**. Cosmos are drought tolerant. Overfertilizing and overwatering can reduce the number of flowers produced. Keep faded blooms cut to encourage more buds. Often, these plants reseed themselves.

### Tips

Cosmos are attractive planted in cottage gardens, at the back of a border or en masse in an informal bed or border. Taller varieties will likely need staking.

### Recommended

*C. bipinnatus* (annual cosmos) has many cultivars. The flowers come in a variety of colors, usually with yellow centers. Old varieties grow tall, while some of the newer cultivars remain quite short. **Sea Shells Series** has flowers in all colors and petals that are rolled into tubes.

Look for *C. atrosanguineus* (chocolate cosmos); on a hot day it smells like chocolate.

*C. bipinnatus* (above & below)

*When cut, cosmos flowers make lovely, long-lasting fillers in arrangements.*

**Features:** white, yellow, gold, orange, pink, red flowers; fern-like foliage **Height:** 1–6' **Spread:** 12–18"

# Cup Flower
## *Nierembergia*

N. hippomanica var. violacea 'Mont Blanc' (above), N. frutescens 'Purple Robe' (below)

The flowers of this plant float like stars atop fern-like foliage. Cup flower is lovely for planting under roses and other complementary flowering shrubs.

### Growing
Cup flower grows well in **full sun** or **partial shade**. It does best in the cooler part of the garden where there is protection from the afternoon sun. The soil should be of **average fertility**, **moist** and **well drained**.

Cup flower is a perennial but is considered an annual in Kansas. During a mild year, it may survive winter. Unfortunately, it may also suffer during the heat of summer. If your plant survives winter, take it as a bonus. However, it is often easier to start new plants each year than to overwinter mature plants.

### Tips
Use cup flower as a groundcover, for edging beds and borders, and for rock gardens, rock walls, containers and hanging baskets. It grows best when summers are cool, and it can withstand a light frost.

### Recommended
*N. frutescens* **'Purple Robe'** is a dense, compact plant that bears purple flowers with golden centers.

*N. hippomanica* var. *violacea* (*N. caerulea*) forms a small mound of foliage. This plant bears delicate, cup-shaped flowers in lavender blue with yellow centers. **'Mont Blanc'** is an All-America Selections winner that bears white flowers with yellow centers.

**Features:** blue, purple, white flowers, yellow centers; habit and foliage **Height:** 6–12" **Spread:** 6–12"

# Fan Flower

*Scaevola*

S. aemula (above & below)

Fan flower's intriguing one-sided flowers add interest to hanging baskets, planters and window boxes.

## Growing

Fan flower grows well in **full sun** or **light shade**. The soil should be of **average fertility, moist** and **very well drained**. Water regularly because this plant doesn't like to dry out completely. It does, however, recover quickly from wilting when watered.

## Tips

Fan flower is a popular choice for hanging baskets and containers, but it can also be used along the tops of rock walls and in rock gardens where it will trail down. This plant makes an interesting addition to mixed borders and it can be planted under shrubs, where the long, trailing stems will form an attractive groundcover.

Fan flower responds well to pinching and trimming. Frequently pinching the tips or trimming the entire plant back will keep it bushy and blooming.

## Recommended

*S. aemula* forms a mound of foliage from which trailing stems emerge. The fan-shaped flowers come in shades of purple, usually with white bases. The species is rarely grown because there are many improved cultivars, which are readily available at your local garden center.

*Given the right conditions, this Australian plant will flower profusely from spring through to frost.*

**Features:** uniquely colored flowers, trailing habit **Height:** up to 8" **Spread:** up to 2'

# Geranium
## *Pelargonium*

Tough, predictable, sun-loving and drought resistant, geraniums have earned their place as flowering favorites in the annual garden. If you are looking for something out of the ordinary, seek out the scented geraniums with their fragrant and often decorative foliage.

## Growing

Geraniums prefer **full sun** but will tolerate partial shade, though they may not bloom as profusely. The soil should be **fertile** and **well drained**.

Deadheading is essential to keep geraniums blooming and looking neat.

## Tips

Geraniums are very popular annual plants, used in borders, beds, planters, hanging baskets and window boxes.

Geraniums are perennials that are treated as annuals and can be kept indoors over winter in a bright room.

## Recommended

*P.* x *hortorum* (bedding geranium, zonal geranium) grows up to 24" tall and 12" wide. Dwarf selections grow up to 8" tall and 6" wide. The flowers are red, pink, purple, orange or white. A wide variety of series are available with variable foliage shape and color, heat tolerance, early-blooming capabilities and flower color.

*P. peltatum* (ivy geranium) has thick, waxy leaves and a trailing habit. Many cultivars are available in a wide variety of flower colors.

*P.* **species** and **cultivars** (scented geraniums, scented pelargoniums) is a large group of geraniums that have scented

*P.* x *hortorum* Fireworks Collection (above)
*P. peltatum* (below)

leaves. The scents are grouped into the categories of rose, mint, citrus, fruit, spice, floral, woodsy and pungent.

*Ivy geranium is one of the most beautiful plants to include in a mixed hanging basket.*

**Features:** colorful flowers; decorative or scented foliage; variable habits
**Height:** 8–24" **Spread:** 6–48"

# Impatiens
*Impatiens*

*I. walleriana* (above), *I. hawkeri* (below)

*The English named* I. walleriana *'busy Lizzie' because it flowers continuously through the growing season.*

Impatiens are the high-wattage darlings of the shade garden, delivering masses of flowers in a wide variety of colors.

## Growing

Impatiens do best in **partial shade** or **light shade** but tolerate full shade or, if kept moist, full sun. New Guinea impatiens are the best adapted to sunny locations. The soil should be **fertile, humus rich, moist** and **well drained**.

## Tips

Impatiens are known for their ability to grow and flower profusely even in shade. Mass plant them in beds under trees, along shady fences or walls or in porch planters. They also look lovely in hanging baskets. New Guinea impatiens are grown as much for their variegated leaves as for their flowers.

## Recommended

*I. hawkeri* (New Guinea hybrids; New Guinea impatiens) bear flowers in shades of red, orange, pink, purple or white. The foliage is sometimes variegated with a yellow stripe down the center of each leaf.

*I. walleriana* (impatiens, busy Lizzie) has flowers in shades of purple, red, burgundy, pink, yellow, salmon, orange, apricot and white and can be bicolored. Dozens of cultivars are available.

*The botanical name for impatiens was once* I. sultani, *after the Sultan of Zanzibar, from whose cool, moist lands this plant originated.*

**Also called:** busy Lizzie **Features:** colorful flowers, grows well in shade
**Height:** 6–36" **Spread:** 12–24"

# Lantana

*Lantana*

These low-maintenance plants, with their stunning flowers, thrive in hot weather and won't suffer if you forget to water them.

## Growing

Lantana grows best in **full sun** but tolerates partial shade. The soil should be **fertile, moist** and **well drained**. Plants are heat and drought tolerant. Cuttings can be taken in late summer and grown indoors for the winter so you will have plants the following summer.

## Tips

Lantana is a tender shrub that is grown as an annual. It makes an attractive addition to beds and borders as well as in mixed containers and hanging baskets.

## Recommended

**L. camara** is a bushy plant that bears round clusters of flowers in a variety of colors. The flowers often change color as they mature, giving flower clusters a striking, multi-colored appearance. Good examples of this are **'Feston Rose,'** which has flowers that open yellow and mature to bright pink, and **'Radiation,'** which bears flowers that open yellow and mature to red. Trailing varieties are also available.

*L. camara* cultivar (above), *L. camara* 'Radiation' (below)

*Lantana will attract butterflies.*

*These shrubby annuals grow quickly and make a stunning addition to mixed planters, combining well with geraniums and other heat-tolerant annuals.*

**Also called:** shrub verbena
**Features:** stunning, colorful flowers
**Height:** 18–24"   **Spread:** up to 4'

# Licorice Plant

*Helichrysum*

*H. petiolare* 'Petite Licorice' (above), *H. petiolare* 'Limelight' (below)

The silvery sheen of licorice plant is caused by a fine, soft pubescence on the leaves. It is a perfect complement to other plants, because silver is the ultimate blending color.

## Growing

Licorice plant prefers **full sun**. The soil should be of **poor to average fertility** and **well drained**. Licorice plant wilts when the soil dries but revives quickly once watered. If it outgrows its space, snip it back with a pair of pruners, shears or even scissors.

## Tips

Licorice plant is a perennial that is grown as an annual and it is prized for its foliage rather than its flowers. Include it in your hanging baskets, planters and window boxes to provide a soft, silvery backdrop for the colorful flowers of other plants. Licorice plant can also be used as a groundcover in beds, borders, rock gardens and along the tops of retaining walls.

## Recommended

*H. petiolare* is a trailing plant with fuzzy, gray-green leaves. Cultivars are more common than the species and include varieties with lime green, silver or variegated leaves.

**Features:** trailing habit; colorful, fuzzy foliage **Height:** 20" **Spread:** about 36"; sometimes up to 6'

# Lobelia
*Lobelia*

*L*obelia adds color to shady spots and blends well with begonias and other colorful shade-loving plants. Lobelia also does well in the sun. Lobelias and marigolds make a striking combination.

## Growing
Lobelia grows best in **partial shade to full shade,** in **fertile, moist, fairly well-drained** soil high in **organic matter**. Lobelia likes cool summer nights. Ensure that its soil stays moist in hot weather. Plant out after the last frost.

Because seedlings are prone to damping off, be sure to use good, clean, seed-starting soil mix. Damping-off causes plants to rot at the soil level, flop over and die.

## Tips
Use lobelia along the edges of beds and borders, on rock walls, in rock gardens, mixed containers and hanging baskets.

Trim lobelia back after its first wave of flowers. This helps ensure the plant flowers through summer. In hot areas, lobelia may die back over summer, but it usually revives as the weather cools.

## Recommended
*L. erinus* may be rounded and bushy, or low and trailing. Many cultivars are available in both forms in shades of purple, blue, pink, white or red. Newer selections including the **Laguna Series** bloom for a longer period.

*L. erinus* cultivars (above & below)

*These lovely plants from the bellflower family contain deadly alkaloids; people have used lobelia as herbal medicine, but it can be poisonous.*

**Features:** abundant, colorful flowers
**Height:** 3–9"  **Spread:** 6" or wider

# Marigold
*Tagetes*

T. patula 'Boy Series' (above), T. patula hybrid (below)

*T. tenuifolia is used as a culinary or tea herb in some Latin American countries, and its petals add a piquant note to a salad.*

$\mathcal{F}$rom the large, exotic, ruffled flowers of African marigold to the tiny flowers on the low-growing signet marigold, the warm colors and fresh scent of marigolds add a festive touch to the garden.

## Growing
Marigolds grow best in **full sun**. The soil should be of **average fertility** and **well drained**. These plants are drought tolerant and hold up well in windy, rainy weather. Sow seed directly in the garden after the chance of frost has passed. Deadhead to prolong blooming and to keep plants tidy.

## Tips
Mass planted or mixed with other plants, marigolds make a vibrant addition to beds, borders and container gardens. These plants will thrive in the hottest, driest parts of your garden.

## Recommended
There are many cultivars available. *T. erecta* (African marigold, American marigold, Aztec marigold) are the largest plants with the biggest flowers; *T. patula* (French marigold) is low growing and has a wide range of flower colors; *T. tenuifolia* (signet marigold) has become more popular recently because of its feathery foliage and small, dainty flowers; *T. Triploid Hybrids* (triploid marigold), developed by crossing French and African marigolds, have huge flowers and compact growth.

**Features:** brightly colored, fiery flowers; fragrant foliage **Height:** 6–36"
**Spread:** 12–24"

# Million Bells
*Calibrachoa*

Million bells is charming, and given the right conditions, it will bloom continually during the growing season with no need to deadhead.

## Growing
Million bells prefers **full sun**. The soil should be **fertile, moist** and **well drained**. Although it prefers to be watered regularly, million bells is fairly drought resistant once established. The flowers develop hardiness as the weather cools, enabling them to bloom well into autumn. Million bells can survive temperatures as low as 20° F.

## Tips
A popular choice for planters and hanging baskets, million bells is also attractive in beds and borders. It grows all summer and needs plenty of room to spread or it will overtake other flowers. Pinch back to keep plants compact if necessary.

## Recommended
*Calibrachoa* hybrids have a dense, trailing habit. They bear small flowers that closely resemble miniature petunias. Cultivars are available in a wide range of flower colors, including striking bicolored varieties. The peach-colored **'Terra Cotta'** looks great paired with intensely colored foliage plants in clay pots.

C. Million Bells Series 'Terra Cotta' (above)
C. Superbells Series 'Trailing Pink' (below)

*The flowers of million bells close at night and on cloudy days.*

**Also called:** trailing petunia
**Features:** colorful flowers; trailing, compact habit **Height:** 6–12" **Spread:** Up to 24"

# Ornamental Pepper
*Capsicum*

C. annuum (above & right)

*I*t's not always necessary to rely on the beauty of flowers when planting annuals. Ornamental peppers flower, but the colorful fruit is sure to catch everyone's attention.

## Growing

Ornamental peppers are as fond of **full sun** as their less ornate counterparts are. The soil should be **moist, fertile, well drained** and rich with organic amendments such as compost. Don't let the soil dry out during hotter periods of the summer, causing the plants to wilt—the result will be stunted growth and little to no fruit.

Seedlings shouldn't be planted until the soil has warmed up in late spring.

## Tips

For maximum impact, plant ornamental peppers in groups or en masse, so they're not lost among other plants as single specimens. They work well in mixed borders and decorative containers. Ornamental peppers should be planted with plants that have flower and foliage colors that complement the pepper's fruit color.

## Recommended

*C. annuum* closely resembles peppers that are grown strictly for their fruit but is often slightly smaller. It bears small, almost inconspicuous white or yellow flowers, followed by shiny, conical fruit. The fruits emerge in pale cream and yellow but slowly mature into shades of purple, orange, yellow and red. The species isn't often available, but many cultivars are on the market with spherical fruit, variegated foliage and varied fruit colors. **'Black Pearl,'** winner of both the 2005 Fleuroselect Quality Mark and a 2006 All-America Selections Award, produces pure black foliage and fruit that matures from black to deep red. **'Jigsaw'** produces colorful, variegated foliage and carmine to purple fruit, and **'Chilly-Chili,'** a 2002 All-America Selections winner, is a compact plant that bears 2" long, red-colored fruit.

**Features:** colorful, shiny, waxy fruit; form, habit **Height:** 6–36" **Spread:** 6–24"

# Ornamental Sweet Potato Vine

*Ipomoea*

This vigorous, rambling plant with lime green, bruised purple or green, pink and cream variegated leaves can make any gardener look like a genius.

## Growing

Grow ornamental sweet potato vine in **full sun to partial shade**. Any type of soil will do but a **light, well-drained** soil of **poor fertility** is preferred.

## Tips

Ornamental sweet potato vine is a great addition to mixed planters, window boxes and hanging baskets. In a rock garden it will spread nicely, and along the top of a retaining wall it will cascade over the edge.

Although this plant is a vine, its bushy habit and colorful leaves make it a useful foliage plant.

## Recommended

*I. batatas* is a twining climber that is grown for its attractive foliage rather than its flowers. Cultivars come in a wide variety of leaf colors. A few of the most popular in Kansas are **'Blackie,'** **'Margarita'** and **'Tri-color.'**

*I. batatas* 'Blackie' (above)
*I. batatas* 'Margarita' (below)

*As a bonus, when you pull up your plant at the end of summer, you can eat any tubers (sweet potatoes) that have formed.*

---

**Also called:** sweet potato vine
**Features:** decorative foliage
**Height:** about 12" **Spread:** up to 10'

# Pentas

*Pentas*

P. lanceolata 'New Look Red' (above)
P. lanceolata (below)

*Pentas is the perfect alternative to geraniums in less traditional container plantings.*

This plant is a welcome addition to the annual or butterfly garden not only for its pretty flowers but also because it prefers not to be watered too often—ideal for those gardeners who aren't very diligent about watering.

## Growing

Pentas grows best in **full sun**. The soil should be **fertile**, **moist** and **well drained**. Deadhead to encourage continuous flowering and to keep plants looking tidy. Pinch plants to encourage bushy growth.

## Tips

Pentas makes a lovely addition to mixed or herbaceous beds and borders. The coarse, dark foliage creates a good background against which brightly colored flowers stand out. It can also be grown in containers, and cuttings taken in late summer can be grown indoors for the winter.

## Recommended

*P. lanceolata* is a subshrub that is grown as an annual. It has an erect or occasionally prostrate habit. Red, pink, purple or white flowers are produced in clusters. Cultivars are available, including **Butterfly Series** that produces flowers in light pink to white, cherry red and hot cherry red with a white eye, deep pink, light lavender and bright red. **New Look Series** offers selections in solid colors of white, red, rose, pink and violet.

**Also called:** star clusters, Egyptian star
**Features:** colorful flowers; foliage
**Height:** 24–36" **Spread:** 24–36"

# Perilla
*Perilla*

Perilla has been used for centuries as a medicinal plant in Chinese medicine and as an Asian culinary herb. Recently, more decorative selections of perilla have been introduced into the market, and it is now a highly sought after bedding plant for gardeners throughout the state.

## Growing
Perilla prefers **full sun** or **partial shade.** The soil should be **fertile** and **moist** but **well drained.** Soil amended with compost or well-composted manure is of added benefit.

## Tips
Perilla is the perfect alternative to coleus and is an ideal complement to both brightly colored annuals and perennials in decorative containers and mixed beds. Perilla is also said to be a good companion plant to tomatoes, repelling bad insects. Planting this annual near or beside your vegetable garden or tomato plants will not only be beneficial but will also beautify the immediate area with color.

## Recommended
*P. frutescens* (perilla, shiso) is a vigorous annual with deeply toothed, mid-green leaves with flecks of purple. The leaves have a cinnamon-lemon flavor. It bears tiny white flowers on spikes, but this annual is grown more for its ornate and colorful foliage. Cultivars are often more popular than the species for ornamental purposes, including **'Magilla'** ('Magilla Purple'), bearing multi-colored leaves of purple, green, white and pink, and **'Magilla Vanilla,'** which is white and green. The leaves may burn in full sun.

---

**Also called:** magilla perilla
**Features:** colorful, ornate foliage; habit
**Height:** 12–30" **Spread:** 12–20"

P. frutescens (above), P. 'Magilla' (below)

*Perilla is well known for its tolerance to the summer heat and will easily compete with some of the most aggressive annuals available.*

# Persian Shield

*Strobilanthes*

S. dyerianus (above & below)

Persian shield's iridescent foliage in shades of purple, bronze, silver and pink adds a bright touch to any annual planting.

## Growing

Persian shield grows well in **full sun** or **partial shade**. The soil should be **average to fertile, light** and **very well**

*Persian shield can be overwintered indoors in a cool, bright location.*

**drained**. Pinch the growing tips to encourage bushy growth. Cuttings can be started in late summer and over-wintered indoors.

## Tips

The colorful foliage of Persian shield provides a dramatic background in annual or mixed beds and borders or in container plantings. Combine this plant with yellow- or white-flowered plants for stunning contrast.

## Recommended

*S. dyerianus* forms a mound of silver- or purple-flushed foliage with contrasting dark green, bronze or purple veins and margins. Spikes of blue flowers may appear in early fall.

**Features:** decorative foliage
**Height:** 18–36"  **Spread:** 24–36"

# Petunia

*Petunia*

*P. 'Purple Wave' (above), P. multiflora type (below)*

For speedy growth, prolific blooming and ease of care, petunias are hard to beat.

## Growing

Petunias prefer **full sun**. The soil should be of **average to rich fertility, light, sandy** and **well drained**. Pinch leggy selections halfway back in mid-summer to keep plants bushy and to encourage new growth and flowers.

## Tips

Use petunias in beds, borders, containers and hanging baskets.

## Recommended

*P.* x *hybrida* is a large group of popular, sun-loving annuals that fall into three categories: **Grandifloras** have the largest flowers in the widest range of colors, but they can be damaged by rain; **Multifloras** bear more flowers that are smaller and less easily damaged by heavy rain; and **Millifloras** have the smallest flowers in the narrowest range of colors, but this type is the most prolific and least likely to be damaged by heavy rain.

*The development of exciting new selections, such as the Supertunia hybrids and Wave Series, has rekindled interest in petunias. These continuously blooming, vigorously spreading, dense-growing hybrids tolerate wet weather and offer tremendous options for hanging baskets, containers and borders.*

**Features:** pink, purple, red, white, yellow, coral, blue or bicolored flowers; versatile plants **Height:** 6–18" **Spread:** 12–24" or wider

# Rose Moss
*Portulaca*

*P. grandiflora* (above & below)

*These plants will fill a sunny, exposed, narrow strip of soil next to pavement with bright colors all summer. They require only minimal attention.*

For a brilliant show in the hottest, driest, most sunbaked and neglected area of the garden, you can't go wrong with rose moss.

## Growing
Rose moss requires **full sun**. The soil should be of **poor fertility, sandy** and **well drained**. To ensure that you have plants where you want them, start seed indoors. If you sow directly outdoors, the tiny seeds may get washed away by rain and the self-seeding plants will pop up in unexpected places. This often occurs, but new seedlings can be transplanted as needed.

## Tips
Rose moss is the ideal plant for garden spots that just don't get enough water, such as under the eaves of a house or in dry, rocky, exposed areas along pathways and in rock walls. It is also an ideal plant for people who like baskets hung from the front porch but sometimes neglect to water them.

## Recommended
*P. grandiflora* forms a bushy mound of succulent foliage. It bears delicate, silky, rose-like single or double flowers profusely all summer. Many cultivars are available, including those with flowers that stay open on cloudy days. **'Calypso Mix'** and the **Sunglo Series** are fine examples of available selections for Kansas.

**Also called:** moss rose, purslane
**Features:** colorful, drought- and heat-resistant flowers **Height:** 4–8" **Spread:** 6–12" or wider

# Salvia
*Salvia*

Salvias should be part of every annual garden. The attractive and varied forms have something to offer every style of garden.

## Growing
All salvia plants prefer **full sun** but tolerate light shade. The soil should be **moist** and **well drained** and of **average to rich fertility,** with lots of **organic matter**.

## Tips
Salvias look good grouped in beds and borders and in containers. The flowers are long lasting and make good cut flowers for arrangements.

To keep plants producing flowers, water often and fertilize monthly.

## Recommended
*S. farinacea* (mealy cup sage, blue sage) has bright blue flowers clustered along stems powdered with silver. Cultivars are available.

*S. splendens* (salvia, scarlet sage) is grown for its spikes of bright red, tubular flowers. Recently, cultivars have become available in white, pink, purple and orange.

S. *splendens* (above), S. *farinacea* 'Victoria' (below)

*There are over 900 species of Salvia.*

**Also called:** sage **Features:** red, blue, purple, burgundy, pink, orange, salmon, yellow, cream, white or bicolored summer flowers; attractive foliage **Height:** 8–48" **Spread:** 8–48"

# Verbena
*Verbena*

*V. x hybrida* (above & below)

Verbenas offer butterflies a banquet. Butterfly visitors include tiger swallowtails, silver-spotted skippers, great spangled fritillaries and painted ladies.

## Growing
Verbenas grow best in **full sun**. The soil should be **fertile** and **very well drained**. Pinch back young plants for bushy growth.

## Tips
Use verbenas on rock walls and in beds, borders, rock gardens, containers, hanging baskets and window boxes. They make good substitutes for ivy-leaved geraniums where the sun is hot and where a roof overhang keeps the mildew-prone verbenas dry.

## Recommended
*V. x **hybrida*** is a bushy plant that may be upright or spreading. It bears clusters of small flowers in a wide range of colors. Cultivars are available.

*The Romans, it is said, believed verbena could rekindle the flames of dying love. They named it* Herba veneris, *'plant of Venus.'*

---

**Also called:** garden verbena
**Features:** summer flowers in shades of red, pink, purple, blue, yellow, scarlet, silver, peach or white; some with white centers
**Height:** 8–60" **Spread:** 12–36"

# Vinca

*Catharanthus*

*C. roseus* (above & below)

Vinca's adaptability makes it a sure-fire winner. It has cheerful flowers, amazing heat tolerance and the ability to bloom happily despite exposure to exhaust fumes and dust. It is one of the best annuals to use in front of homes and businesses on busy streets.

## Growing

Vinca prefers **full sun** but tolerates partial shade. **Well-drained** soil is necessary because vinca is prone to root rot. This plant tolerates pollution and drought but prefers to be watered regularly. It doesn't like to be too wet or too cold. Plant vinca after the soil has warmed and don't replant it where it has gotten root rot in the past.

**Also called:** Madagascar periwinkle
**Features:** attractive foliage; shades of red, pink, purple, white, apricot flowers, often with contrasting centers; durable plants
**Height:** 10–24" **Spread:** usually equal to or greater than height

## Tips

Vinca will do well in the sunniest, warmest part of the garden. Plant it in a bed along an exposed driveway or against the south-facing wall of the house. It can also be used in hanging baskets, in planters and as a temporary groundcover.

## Recommended

*C. roseus* (*Vinca rosea*) forms a mound of strong stems. The flowers are pink, red or white, often with contrasting centers. Many cultivars are available. **Cooler Series** plants have light-colored flowers with darker, contrasting centers and **Pacifica Series** has flowers in various colors on compact plants.

# Zinnia

*Zinnia*

Z. angustifolia 'Classic' (above), Z. elegans (below)

The brightly colored, long stemmed flowers make excellent long lasting additions to fresh arrangements and summer bouquets.

## Growing

Zinnias grow best in **full sun**. The soil should be **fertile**, rich in **organic matter, moist** and **well drained**. It's best to directly sow zinnia seeds into your beds, however, when starting seeds indoors, plant them in individual peat pots to avoid disturbing the roots when transplanting.

Deadhead zinnias to keep them flowering and looking their best. To keep mildew from the leaves and botrytis blight from the flowers, plant varieties that are resistant to these problems and avoid wetting the plants when you water.

## Tips

Zinnias are useful in beds, borders, containers and cutting gardens. The dwarf varieties can be used as edging plants. These plants are wonderful for fall color. Combine the rounded zinnia flowers with the spiky blooms of sun-loving salvia, or use the taller varieties in front of taller annuals and perennials.

## Recommended

*Z. angustifolia* (narrow-leaf zinnia) is a low, mounding plant that bears yellow and orange flowers.

*Z. elegans* and its cultivars bear flowers in several forms including single, double and cactus flowered, where the petals appear to be rolled into tubes like the spines of a cactus. **'Zowie! Yellow Flame,'** a 2006 All-America Selections winner, produces fiery colored, double flowers.

*Z.* **Profusion Series** includes fast-growing, mildew-resistant hybrids. This series is an All-America Selections Winner and is considered to be the best bedding zinnias available.

**Features:** brightly colored flowers; dense growth habit **Height:** 6–36" **Spread:** 12"

# Aster

*Aster*

Native asters, such as *A. novae-angliae*, decorate our roadsides in fall. Their cultivated counterparts are richer in color, larger in bloom and somewhat better behaved.

## Growing

Asters prefer **full sun** but benefit from some afternoon shade to keep them from suffering in August's heat and humidity. The soil should be **fertile, moist** and **well drained**. Pinch plants back several times before mid-July to promote dense growth and to reduce disease problems such as mildew. Mulch in winter to protect plants from temperature fluctuations. Divide every two or three years to maintain vigor and control spread.

## Tips

Use asters in the middle of borders and in cottage gardens, or naturalize them in wild gardens. The purple and pink flowers contrast nicely with the yellow-flowered perennials common in the late-summer garden.

## Recommended

Some aster species have been reclassified under the genus *Symphyotrichum*. You may see both names at garden centers. Many cultivars are available.

**A. dumosus** (bushy aster) grows 12–18" in height and produces white or lavender flowers with yellow centers.

**A. novae-angliae** (Michaelmas daisy, New England aster) is an upright, spreading, clump-forming perennial that bears yellow-centered, purple flowers.

*A. novae-angliae* (above), *A. novi-belgii* (below)

**A. novi-belgii** (Michaelmas daisy, New York aster) is a dense, upright, clump-forming perennial with purple flowers.

**Features:** red, white, blue, purple, pink late-summer to mid-fall flowers, often with yellow centers  **Height:** 7"–5'  **Spread:** 18–36"  **Hardiness:** zones 3–8

# Beebalm

*Monarda*

*M. didyma* 'Marshall's Delight' (above)
*M. didyma* (below)

Bees and butterflies flock to a garden that has a well-grown stand of beebalm.

## Growing

Beebalm grows well in **full sun, partial shade** or **light shade** in **humus-rich, moist, well-drained** soil of **average fertility**. Divide every two or three years in spring just as new growth emerges.

In June, cut back some of the stems by half to extend the flowering period and to encourage compact growth. Thinning the stems also helps prevent powdery mildew. If mildew strikes after flowering, cut the plants back to 6" to increase air circulation.

## Tips

Use beebalm beside a stream or pond, or in a lightly shaded, well-watered border. It spreads in moist, fertile soils, but roots close to the surface can be removed easily.

Using pesticides can be harmful to bees and butterflies and makes it unsuitable for culinary or medicinal purposes.

## Recommended

*M. didyma* is a bushy, mounding plant that forms a thick clump of stems with red or pink flowers. Newer cultivars are resistant to mildew and come in a variety of sizes, colors and forms.

*As the name suggests, beebalm is extremely attractive to bees, hummingbirds and other pollinators. This plant is a source of nectar for butterflies.*

**Also called:** bergamot, Oswego tea
**Features:** fragrant blossoms in shades of red, pink, purple, white **Height:** 9–40"
**Spread:** 2–4' **Hardiness:** zones 3–8

# Black-Eyed Susan

*Rudbeckia*

The cultivar 'Goldsturm' is an excellent anchor perennial because of its long life, bright yellow flowers and long blooming season. It won't die out in the center and won't encroach on its neighbors.

## Growing

Black-eyed Susan grows well in **full sun** or **partial shade**. The soil should be of **average fertility** and **well drained**. Several *Rudbeckia* species are touted as 'claybusters' because they tolerate fairly heavy clay soils. Established plants are drought tolerant, but regular watering is best. Divide in spring every three to five years.

## Tips

Black-eyed Susan is a tough, low-maintenance, enduring perennial. Plant it wherever you want a casual look. It looks great planted in drifts. Include these native plants in wildflower and natural gardens, beds and borders. Pinching the plants in spring will result in shorter, bushier stands.

## Recommended

*R. fulgida* is an upright, spreading plant bearing orange-yellow flowers with brown centers. **Var.** *sullivantii* **'Goldsturm'** bears large, bright, golden yellow flowers. **'Irish Eyes'** has a green center.

*R. hirta* **'Cherokee Sunset'** grows 24" tall and 12" wide, bearing multi-colored, fiery flowers with dark mahogany centers, in semi-double and double forms.

*R. nitida* (shining coneflower) **'Herbstsonne'** grows to 7' and has bright golden yellow, ray flowers with a green center.

**Features:** bright yellow, orange, red midsummer to fall flowers with brown or green centers; attractive foliage; easy to grow
**Height:** 18"–10' **Spread:** 12–36"
**Hardiness:** zones 3–9

*R. fulgida* (above)
*R. nitida* 'Herbstsonne' (below)

*The flowers last well when cut for arrangements.*

# Blue-Mist Shrub
## *Caryopteris*

Blue-mist shrub is cultivated for its aromatic stems, foliage and flowers. A few cut stems in a vase will delicately scent a room. Blue-mist shrub is also a favorite of butterflies and bees.

### Growing

Blue-mist shrub prefers **full sun**, but it tolerates light shade. It does best in soil of **average fertility** that is **light** and **well drained**. Wet and poorly drained soils can kill this plant. Blue-mist shrub is very drought tolerant once established. It can die back during cold winters. Cut back the dead growth in spring, or prune the plant to about 6" tall. New shoots will sprout from the base, producing late-summer flowers.

### Tips

Include blue-mist shrub in your shrub or mixed border. The bright blue, late-season flowers are welcome when many other plants are past their flowering best.

### Recommended

*C.* x *clandonensis* grows into a dense mound that grows up to 3' tall and 3–5' in spread. It bears clusters of blue or purple flowers in late summer and early fall. Cultivars are more often grown than the species, but not all are hardy across Kansas. 'First Choice' is hardy to Zone 5 and is more compact than others.

*The name* Caryopteris *is derived from the Greek* karyon *(nut) and* pteron *(wing), referring to the winged fruit.*

C. x *clandonensis cultivar* (above)
C. x *clandonensis* (below)

**Also called:** bluebeard, blue spirea
**Features:** rounded, spreading, deciduous shrub; attractive, fragrant foliage, twigs and late-summer flowers **Height:** 2–4'
**Spread:** 2–5' **Hardiness:** zones 5–9

# Butterfly Bush

*Buddleia*

*B. davidii* (above & below)

This willowy bush with its fragrant flowers will attract countless butterflies along with a wide variety of other pollinating insects.

## Growing

Butterfly bushes prefer to grow in **full sun**, producing few if any flowers in shady conditions. The soil should be of **average fertility** and **well drained**. Plants are drought tolerant once established. Plants flower on the current year's growth so cut them back to 6" in late winter and they will still produce blooms. They are one of the last plants to leaf out in spring.

## Tips

Butterfly bushes make beautiful additions to shrub and mixed borders. The graceful arching habit makes them ideal as specimen plants. The dwarf forms that stay under 5' are suitable for small gardens.

## Recommended

*B. davidii* (orange-eye butterfly bush, summer lilac) is the most commonly grown species. It grows 4–10' tall, with an equal spread. It bears fragrant flowers in bright and pastel shades of purple, pink, blue or white from mid-summer through fall. Many cultivars are available.

*B. weyeriana* is a wide-spreading shrub with arching stems. It grows 6–12' tall, spreads 5–10' and bears purple or yellow flowers from mid-summer through fall. Cultivars are available.

---

**Features:** large, deciduous shrub with arching branches, attractive flowers, habit and foliage **Height:** 4–12' **Spread:** 4–10'
**Hardiness:** zones 5–9

# Butterfly Weed
## *Asclepias*

A. incarnata (above), A. tuberosa (below)

Native to North America, butterfly weed attracts butterflies, most notably the monarch butterfly—it is the major food source for the species.

### Growing
Butterfly weed grows best in **full sun**. The soil should be **fertile, moist** and **well drained,** although *A. tuberosa* is drought tolerant. To propagate, the seedlings can be transplanted as needed, but mature plants resent being divided.

Deadhead to encourage a second flush of blooms.

### Tips
Use *A. tuberosa* in meadow plantings and borders, on dry banks, in neglected areas and in wildflower, cottage-style and butterfly gardens. Use *A. incarnata* in moist borders and in bog, pondside or stream-side plantings.

### Recommended
**A. incarnata** (swamp milkweed) forms a dense clump of thick stems that bear clusters of pink, white or light purple flowers in late spring or early summer. Cultivars are available.

**A. tuberosa** (butterfly weed) forms a clump of upright, leafy stems. It bears clusters of orange flowers from mid-summer to early fall. Cultivars are available.

*Tender and annual species of* Asclepias *are also available. A popular species is* A. curassavica *(blood flower), with red, orange or yellow flowers that last all summer.*

**Also called:** milkweed, pleurisy root
**Features:** late-spring, summer and early-fall flowers in red, yellow, orange, white, pink or light purple; attracts butterflies
**Height:** 18"–5' **Spread:** 12–24"
**Hardiness:** zones 4–9

# Catmint

*Nepeta*

Real workhorses in the garden bed, catmints offer season-long blooms on sturdy, trouble-free plants.

## Growing

These plants prefer **full sun** or **partial shade**. Grow them in **well-drained** soil of **average fertility**; the growth tends to flop in rich soil. Plant them in spring. Divide overgrown and dense plants in spring or fall.

In June, pinch the tips to delay flowering and make the plants more compact. Shear off spent flowers to encourage a second flush of flowers through fall.

## Tips

Catmints form upright, spreading clumps. Plant them in herb gardens, perennial beds, rock gardens or cottage-style gardens with roses, or use them for edging borders and pathways.

Once cats discover catmint in your garden, it can be difficult to keep them out of it, because they prefer it even to *N. cataria* (catnip).

## Recommended

*N.* **'Blue Beauty'** ('Souvenir d'André Chaudron') has gray-green foliage and large, dark purple-blue flowers.

*N.* **x** *faassenii* bears blue or purple flowers. Cultivars with gray-green foliage and pink, white, light purple or lavender blue flowers are available, as are low-growing cultivars.

*N.* **'Six Hills Giant'** bears deep lavender blue flowers.

Features: aromatic foliage; attractive blue, purple, white or pink flowers; easy to grow **Height:** 6–36" **Spread:** 12–24" **Hardiness:** zones 3–8

*N.* x *faassenii* 'Walker's Low' (above)
*N.* x *faassenii* (below)

*Like all members of the mint family, catmint has square stems.*

# Columbine

*Aquilegia*

*A. canadensis* (above), *A.* x *hybrida* 'McKana Giants' (below)

ainty, intricate columbine flowers nodding above scalloped foliage bring lightness and grace wherever you plant them.

## Growing

Columbines grow best with **morning sun** and **afternoon shade**. They prefer soil that is **fertile, moist** and **well drained** but adapt well to most soil conditions. Division is not required but can be done to propagate desirable plants. The divided plants may take a while to recover because columbines dislike having their roots disturbed.

## Tips

Use columbines in rock gardens, formal or casual borders and naturalized or woodland gardens.

## Recommended

*A. canadensis* (wild columbine, Canada columbine) is a native plant that is common in woodlands and fields. It bears yellow flowers with red spurs.

*A.* x *hybrida* (*A.* x *cultorum*; hybrid columbine) forms mounds of delicate foliage and has exceptional flowers. Many hybrids have been developed with showy flowers in a wide range of colors.

*A. vulgaris* (European columbine, common columbine) has been used to develop many hybrids and cultivars with flowers in a variety of colors. **'Plena'** has double flowers.

**Features:** red, yellow, pink, purple, blue, white spring and summer flowers, color of spurs often differs from that of the petals; attractive foliage **Height:** 7–30" **Spread:** 12–24" **Hardiness:** zones 3–8

# Coneflower

*Echinacea*

This native wildflower version of the shuttlecock has exploded on the garden scene with a range of new colors.

## Growing

Coneflower grows well in **full sun** or very **light shade**. It tolerates any **well-drained** soil, but prefers soil of **average to rich fertility**. The thick taproots make this plant drought resistant, but it prefers to have regular water. Divide every four years or so in spring or fall.

Deadhead early in the season to prolong flowering. Later you may wish to leave the flowerheads in place to self-seed and provide winter interest, or remove the flowers to prevent self-seeding. Pinch plants back or thin out the stems in early summer to encourage bushy growth that will be less prone to mildew.

## Tips

Use coneflowers in meadow gardens and informal borders, either in groups or as single specimens. The dry flowerheads make an interesting feature in fall and winter gardens.

## Recommended

*E. purpurea* is an upright plant covered in prickly hairs. It bears purple flowers with orangy centers. **Big Sky hybrids** are the result of crossing *E. purpurea* and *E. paradoxa*. **'Sundown'** has pink-orange flowers, **'Sunrise'** produces yellow blossoms and **'Twilight'** has pink-red flowers. Other cultivars are available with flower colors in green, white and pink.

---

**Features:** purple, pink, white, orange, green, yellow mid-summer to fall flowers with rusty orange or green centers; persistent seedheads **Height:** 18"–4' **Spread:** 12–24" **Hardiness:** zones 3–8

*E. purpurea* 'Magnus' and 'White Swan' (above)
*E. purpurea* (below)

*Coneflower attracts butterflies and other wildlife to the garden, providing pollen, nectar and seeds to the various hungry visitors.*

# Coral Bells

*Heuchera*

*H. micrantha* 'Palace Purple' (above & below)

These delicate, woodland plants will enhance your garden with their bright colors, attractive foliage and airy sprays of flowers.

## Growing

Coral bells grow best in **light** or **partial shade.** The foliage colors can bleach out in full sun, and plants grow leggy in full shade. The soil should be of **average to rich fertility, humus rich, moist** and **well drained**. Good air circulation is essential.

Deadhead to prolong the bloom. Every two or three years, coral bells should be dug up and the oldest, woodiest roots and stems removed. Plants may be divided at this time, then replanted with the crown at or just above soil level.

## Tips

Use coral bells as edging plants, in clusters and woodland gardens or as groundcovers in low-traffic areas. Combine different foliage types to create an interesting display. Coral bells are also great for containers, where they can survive the winter season outside.

## Recommended

There are dozens of beautiful cultivars available with almost limitless variations of foliage markings and colors. *H. micrantha* **'Palace Purple'** started the fascination with darker foliage coral bells when it won the Perennial Plant of the Year in 1991.

**Also called:** alum root **Features:** very decorative foliage; red, pink, white, yellow, purple spring or summer flowers
**Height:** 1–4' **Spread:** 12–18"
**Hardiness:** zones 3–9

# Coreopsis
*Coreopsis*

*C. verticillata* 'Moonbeam' (above), *C. auriculata* 'Nana' (below)

These plants produce flowers all summer and are easy to grow; they make a fabulous addition to every garden.

## Growing

Coreopsis grows best in **full sun**. The soil should be of **average fertility, sandy, light** and **well drained**. Plants can develop crown rot in moist, cool locations with heavy soil. Too fertile a soil will encourage floppy growth. Deadhead to keep plants blooming or to prevent them from reseeding.

## Tips

Coreopsis is a versatile plant, useful in formal and informal borders and in meadow plantings and cottage gardens. They look best when planted in groups.

## Recommended

*C. auriculata* 'Nana' (mouse-eared tickseed) is a low-growing species, well suited to rock gardens and the fronts of borders. It grows about 12" tall and spreads indefinitely, though slowly. It bears yellow-orange flowers in late spring.

*C. grandiflora* is a clump-forming plant with lance-shaped leaves and solitary, yellow flowers. **'Baby Sun'** is a compact selection and is part of the Prairie Bloom Collection.

*C. verticillata* (thread-leaf coreopsis) is a mound-forming plant with attractive, finely divided foliage and bright yellow flowers. It grows 24–32" tall and spreads 18". Available cultivars include **'Moonbeam,'** which forms a mound of delicate, lacy foliage and bears creamy yellow flowers.

**Also called:** tickseed **Features:** yellow, yellow-orange summer flowers; attractive foliage **Height:** 12–32" **Spread:** 12–24" **Hardiness:** zones 3–9

# Daylily
*Hemerocallis*

With the challenging gardening conditions in the Midwest, we need something that we can count on year after year. There are few garden plants that fit that bill better than daylilies.

## Growing

Daylilies grow in **full sun** but will tolerate light shade. The deeper the shade, the fewer flowers will be produced. The soil should be **fertile, moist** and **well drained**, but these plants adapt to most conditions and are hard to kill once established. Feed in spring and mid-summer for the best flower display. Divide every three to four years in late summer to keep plants vigorous and to propagate them. They can, however, be left indefinitely without dividing.

## Tips

Plant daylilies alone, or group them in borders, on banks and in ditches to control erosion. They can be naturalized in woodland or meadow gardens. Small varieties are nice in planters.

Deadhead to prolong blooming. Be careful when deadheading purple-flowered daylilies because the sap can stain fingers and clothes.

*H. 'Dewey Roquemore' (above), H. 'Bonanza' (below)*

## Recommended

Daylilies come in an almost infinite number of forms, sizes and colors in a range of species, cultivars and hybrids. See your local garden center or daylily grower to find out what's available and most suitable for your garden.

**Features:** spring and summer flowers in every color except blue and pure white; grass-like foliage **Height:** 1–5' **Spread:** 2–4' or more **Hardiness:** zones 2–9

# Dianthus

*Dianthus*

*D. deltoides* (above), *D. plumarius* (below)

The grass-like foliage of dianthus adds a contrasting texture in the front of a border. Dianthus prefer alkaline soils but need good drainage to flourish.

## Growing

Dianthus prefer **full sun** but tolerate some light shade. A **well-drained, neutral or alkaline** soil is required. The most important factor in the successful cultivation of dianthus is drainage—they hate to stand in water. Mix organic matter and gravel into their area of the flowerbed, if needed, to encourage good drainage. Deadhead to prolong blooming.

## Tips

Dianthus make excellent plants for rock gardens and rock walls, and for edging flower borders and walkways. They can also be used in cutting gardens and even as groundcovers.

## Recommended

*D. deltoides* (maiden pink) forms a mat of foliage and flowers in shades of red.

*D. gratianopolitanus* (cheddar pink) is long-lived and forms a very dense mat of evergreen, silver gray foliage with sweet-scented flowers mostly in shades of pink.

*D. plumarius* (cottage pink) is noteworthy for its role in the development of many popular cultivars known collectively as garden pinks. The single, semi-double or fully double flowers are available in many colors.

**Also called:** pinks **Features:** pink, red, white, purple spring or summer flowers; attractive foliage; sometimes fragrant **Height:** 2–18"
**Spread:** 12–24" **Hardiness:** zones 3–9

# Goldenrod

*Solidago*

S. 'Crown of Rays' (above & below)

*Ragweed (Ambrosia species), not goldenrod, is the source of hay-fever pollen.*

The cultivated varieties of goldenrod tame the unruly appearance of the native species but keep the profusion of bloom.

### Growing

Goldenrod prefers **full sun** but tolerates partial shade. The soil should be of **poor to average fertility, light** and **well drained**. Too fertile a soil results in lush growth, few flowers and invasive behavior.

Divide goldenrod every three to five years in spring to keep it vigorous and to control growth.

### Tips

Goldenrod is great for providing late-season color. It looks at home in a large border, cottage-style garden or wild-flower garden. Don't plant it near less vigorous plants, because goldenrod can quickly overwhelm them. Goldenrod is a great plant for xeriscaping.

### Recommended

*Solidago* **hybrids** form a clump of strong stems with narrow leaves. They grow about 2–4' tall and spread about 18–24". Plume-like clusters of yellow flowers are produced from mid-summer to fall. **'Crown of Rays'** holds its flower clusters in horizontal spikes and flowers from mid-summer to fall. **'Fireworks'** has strong, sturdy stems and golden yellow flower spikes that dart horizontally throughout the clump of foliage. **'Golden Shower'** bears flowers in horizontal or drooping plumes.

**Features:** yellow flowers from mid-summer through fall; attractive habit **Height:** 2–4' **Spread:** 18–30" **Hardiness:** zones 3–8

# Hardy Hibiscus

*Hibiscus*

It's always hard to convince people that these oversized, tropical beauties are really perennials that deserve a place in the garden. Although the extremely large flowers last only a single day, deadheading keeps them blooming late into summer.

## Growing

Grow hardy hibiscus in **full sun to afternoon shade**. The soil should be **humus rich, moist** and **well drained**. Hardy hibiscus is a heavy feeder and benefits from a side dressing of fertilizer when it begins to leaf out. Cut back by one-half in early June for bushier, more compact growth and prolonged blooming. Deadhead to keep the plant tidy and blooming. Mark this plant's location in fall because it is slow to emerge in spring.

## Tips

This plant adds interest to the back of an informal border or in a pondside planting. The large flowers create a bold focal point in late-summer gardens.

Hummingbirds are attracted to these plants.

## Recommended

*H. moscheutos* is a large, vigorous plant with strong stems. The huge flowers can be up to 12" across. Cultivars are available, including some wonderful plants such as '**Crown Jewels,**' a short selection with 8" wide, creamy white blossoms; '**Disco Belle Pink**' with huge white flowers that take on a pink blush; '**Kopper King,**' bearing coppery foliage with white flowers streaked hot pink; and '**Lord Baltimore,**' with crimson red flowers.

*H. moscheutos* 'Lord Baltimore' (above)
*H. moscheutos* cultivar (below)

*Because hardy hibiscus is late to emerge in spring, be careful not to overwater its planting site, to prevent the onset of rot.*

**Also called:** rose mallow **Features:** white, red, pink mid-summer to frost flowers
**Height:** 18"–8' **Spread:** 36"
**Hardiness:** zones 4–9

# Hardy Mum
*Chrysanthemum*

C. hybrids (above & below)

*You can deadhead in late fall or early winter, but leave the stems intact to protect the crowns of the plants.*

Hardy mums are excellent plants for 'brown-thumb' gardeners—you can't fail with this one.

### Growing
Hardy mums grow best in **full sun** in **fertile, moist, well-drained** soil. Early planting improves their chances of surviving winter. Many selections, except the 'no-pinch' and cushion hardy chrysanthemums, will produce more flowers and get bushier if they are pinched at 6" tall. Remove the top inch, then do so again following the next 6" of growth, but stop pinching after the middle of July. Divide plants every two years in early spring to keep them growing vigorously.

### Tips
Hardy mums provide a blaze of color in the fall garden. They can be included in borders and planters, or in plantings close to the house. In fall, they can be added to areas where summer annuals have faded.

### Recommended
*Chrysanthemum* hybrids are sturdy, mound-forming perennials that come in a range of sizes, colors and flower forms. There are many varieties available.

*C.* **'Mei-Kyo'** bears pale pink to rich pink, double flowers over a long period.

*C.* **Prophet Series** is popular and commonly available, with flowers blooming in many colors. **'Christine'** has deep salmon pink, double flowers with yellow centers. **'Raquel'** has bright red, double flowers with yellow centers.

**Features:** orange, yellow, pink, red, purple late-summer or fall flowers; habit **Height:** 12–36" **Spread:** 2'–4' **Hardiness:** zones 5–9

# Hens and Chicks

*Sempervivum*

*S. tectorum* 'Limelight' and 'Atropurpureum' (above); *S. tectorum* (below)

The genus name *Sempervivum* means 'always living,' which is appropriate for these fascinating and constantly regenerating plants.

## Growing

Grow hens and chicks in **full sun** or **partial shade**. The soil should be of **poor to average fertility** and **very well drained**. Add fine gravel or grit to the soil to provide adequate drainage. Once a plant blooms, it dies. When you deadhead the faded flower, pull up the soft parent plant as well to provide space for the new daughter rosettes that sprout up, seemingly by magic. Divide by removing these new rosettes and rooting them.

*The little plantlets are simple to pass along. Just separate a 'chick' and you can start a whole colony of plants.*

**Features:** succulent foliage; unusual flowers
**Height:** 3–6"   **Spread:** 12" to indefinite
**Hardiness:** zones 3–8

## Tips

These plants make excellent additions to rock gardens and rock walls, where they will grow even right on the rocks.

## Recommended

**S. tectorum** is one of the most commonly grown hens and chicks. It forms a low-growing mat of fleshy-leaved rosettes, each about 6–10" across. Small new rosettes are quickly produced and grow and multiply to fill almost any space. Flowers may be produced in summer but are not as common in colder climates. The flowers emerge in the summer months in shades of red, yellow, white and purple.

# Hosta

*Hosta*

*H. sieboldiana* 'Elegans' (above)

*Some gardeners think the flowers clash with the foliage. You can remove the flowers when they emerge, if you find them unattractive.*

These shade-loving plants are pretty tough. With an amazing array of leaf colors, textures, sizes and forms, flowering habits and even fragrance, hostas rank as one of our favorite shade plants.

## Growing

Hostas prefer **light** or **partial shade** but will grow in full shade. Morning sun is preferable to afternoon sun. The soil should ideally be **fertile, moist** and **well drained**, but most soils are tolerated. Hostas are fairly drought tolerant, especially if mulch is used to help retain moisture. Division is not required but can be done every few years in spring or summer to propagate new plants.

## Tips

Hostas make wonderful woodland plants and they look very attractive when combined with ferns and other fine-textured plants. Hostas work well in mixed borders, particularly when used to hide the leggy lower stems and branches of some shrubs. Their dense growth and thick, shade-providing leaves help suppress weeds in the garden. Hostas are known to struggle a bit in western Kansas owing to soils with a high pH, lack of shady locations, excessive heat.

## Recommended

There are hundreds of hosta species, cultivars and hybrids.

**Also called:** plantain lily **Features:** decorative foliage; white or purple summer and fall flowers **Height:** 7–36" **Spread:** 2–4' **Hardiness:** zones 3–8

# Iris

*Iris*

Irises come in many shapes, sizes and colors. The most traditional form is the tall, bearded iris.

## Growing

Irises prefer **full sun** but tolerate very light or dappled shade. The soil should be of **average fertility** and **well drained**. Japanese and Siberian iris prefer a moist but well-drained soil. Deadhead irises to keep them tidy. Cut back the foliage of Siberian iris in spring.

Divide irises when the number or size of flowers diminish, in late summer or early fall. Replant bearded iris rhizomes with the flat side of the foliage fan facing the garden, just below the soil surface.

## Tips

All irises are popular border plants. Japanese and Siberian iris grow well alongside streams or ponds. Dwarf cultivars look attractive in rock gardens.

Irises can cause severe internal irritation if ingested. Always wash your hands after handling them. Avoid planting irises where children play.

## Recommended

Many species and hybrids are available. Among the most popular is the bearded iris, often a hybrid of **I. germanica**. It has the widest range of flower colors but is susceptible to attack from the iris borer. Several irises are not susceptible, including Japanese iris (**I. ensata**) and Siberian iris (**I. sibirica**). Check with your local garden center to find out what's available.

*I. sibirica* (above), *I. germanica* 'Stepping Out' (below)

Features: spring, summer and, sometimes, fall flowers in many shades of pink, red, purple, blue, white, brown, yellow; attractive foliage
Height: 6"–4' Spread: 6"–4'
Hardiness: zones 3–10

# Joe Pye Weed
*Eupatorium*

*E. rugosum* (above), *E. purpureum* (below)

*J*f you want a bold, beautiful perennial, here's your chance. Joe Pye weed looks great around lakes and ponds, at the back of borders, and mixed in with tall grasses and prairie plants.

## Growing
Joe Pye weed prefers **full sun** but tolerates partial shade. The soil should be **fertile** and **moist**. Wet soils are tolerated. Divide plants in spring when clumps become overgrown.

Pruning growth back in May encourages branching and lower, denser growth, but it can delay flowering. It may take a couple of seasons for these plants to mature, so don't crowd them.

## Tips
The tall types are ideal in the back of a border or in the center of a bed where they will create a backdrop for lower-growing plants.

## Recommended
*E. purpureum* (sweet Joe Pye weed) is a large, clump-forming native species with domed clusters of pink to purple-pink flowers, purple-tinged stems and large, purple-tinged, mid-green foliage.

*E.rugosum* (*Ageratina altissima*) forms a bushy, mounding clump bearing white flowers.

**Also called:** boneset, white snakeroot
**Features:** attractive foliage; white, purple, blue, pink late summer and fall flowers **Height:** 2–9'
**Spread:** 2–4' **Hardiness:** zones 3–9

# Lamb's Ears

### *Stachys*

Named for its soft, fuzzy leaves, lamb's ears has silvery foliage that is a beautiful contrast to any bold-colored plants that tower above it.

### Growing

Lamb's ears grows best in **full sun**. The soil should be of **poor** or **average fertility** and **well drained**. The leaves can rot in humid weather if the soil is poorly drained. Remove spent flower spikes to keep the plants looking neat.

### Tips

Lamb's ears makes a great groundcover in a new garden where the soil has not yet been amended. When used to edge borders and pathways, it provides a soft, silvery backdrop for more vibrant colors next to it. For a silvery accent, plant a small group of lamb's ears in a border.

### Recommended

**S. byzantina** forms a mat of thick, woolly rosettes of leaves. Pinkish purple flowers bloom in early summer. The species can be quite invasive, so choosing a cultivar may be wise. The many cultivars offer a variety of foliage colors, sizes and flowers. **'Helen von Stein'** ('Big Ears'), is a clump-forming perennial that produces fuzzy leaves twice as large as those of other species or cultivars.

*Many plants in the mint family contain antibacterial and antifungal compounds. Lamb's ears not only feels soft, but it may actually encourage healing.*

S. byzantina 'Big Ears' (above), S. byzantina (below)

**Also called:** lamb's tails, lamb's tongues
**Features:** soft and fuzzy, silver foliage; pink or purple flowers  **Height:** 6–18"
**Spread:** 18–24"  **Hardiness:** zones 3–8

# Peony
*Paeonia*

Peonies, known for their familiar pink 'eyes' and strong roots, have been the backbone of perennial gardens for generations.

## Growing

Peonies prefer **full sun** but tolerate some shade. They like **fertile, humus-rich, moist, well-drained** soil with lots of compost. Prepare the planting hole before introducing the plants by amending the soil with compost or well-composted manure. Mulch peonies lightly with compost in spring. Too much fertilizer, particularly nitrogen, causes floppy growth and retards blooming. Peonies rarely need to be divided but can be divided in early fall for propagation. Deadhead to keep plants looking tidy. Remove any debris from the base of peony plants in fall to reduce the possibility of disease.

## Tips

Peonies look great in a border combined with other early bloomers. Avoid planting peonies under trees, where they have to compete for moisture and nutrients.

Tubers planted too shallowly or, more commonly, too deeply will not flower. The buds or eyes on the tuber should be 1–2" below the soil surface.

Place wire tomato or peony cages around the plants in early spring to support the heavy flowers.

## Recommended

There are hundreds of peonies available. The single or double flowers come in many colors and may be fragrant. Visit your local garden center to see what is available.

*P. lactiflora* 'Shimmering Velvet' (above)
*P. lactiflora* cultivars (below)

**Features:** white, cream white, yellow, pink, red, purple spring and early-summer flowers; attractive foliage **Height:** 24–36" **Spread:** 24–36" **Hardiness:** zones 2–7

# Perennial Salvia

*Salvia*

*S. nemorosa* 'May Night'

*S. x superba* 'Blue Queen'

Perennial salvias are reliable, hardy members of the perennial border.

## Growing

Perennial salvia prefers **full sun** but tolerates light shade. The soil should be of **average fertility, humus rich** and **well drained**. The plants are drought tolerant once established.

Deadhead to prolong blooming. Trim plants back in spring to encourage new growth and to keep them tidy. New shoots will sprout from old, woody growth.

## Tips

Perennial salvias are attractive plants for the middle or front of the border. They can also be grown in mixed planters.

## Recommended

*S. nemorosa* (*S.* x *superba*) is a clump-forming, branching plant with gray-green leaves and spikes of blue or purple summer flowers. Cultivars are available including the highly recommended **'Amethyst,' 'May Night'** and **'Viola Klose.'**

*S.* x *superba* is a clump-forming perennial, in a branched form. It bears bright purple flowers from mid-summer to early fall. **'Blue Queen'** has purple-blue flowers.

---

Also called: meadow sage  Features: attractive, cream, purple, blue, pink flowers; foliage  Height: 24–36"  Spread: 24–36"  Hardiness: zones 5–9

*The genus name,* Salvia, *is Latin for 'save,' referring to the medicinal properties of several species.*

# Persicaria

*Persicaria*

mall, densely packed spikes of colorful flowers cloak these plants in late
summer and fall, providing the late-season
garden with much-needed color.

## Growing

Persicaria grow well in **full sun** and **partial
shade**. Soil should be of **average fertility,
moist** and **well drained**. Established
plants are quite drought tolerant. Divide
in spring or fall when clumps begin to
thin out in the center.

## Tips

Persicaria make good additions to low-
maintenance beds and borders. White
fleeceflower makes a majestic backdrop
plant and can be mass planted to create a
billowy deciduous screen.

## Recommended

*P. polymorpha* (white fleeceflower) is a
tall, clump-forming perennial that bears
large clusters of creamy white flowers.
Plants grow 3–4' tall and 3' wide.

*P. virginiana* is an upright perennial
bearing mid-green leaves with dark
green markings. Inconspicuous flowers
emerge in late summer. This species can
grow 18–48" in height and 24–56" wide,
and has the tendency to grow aggres-
sively to the point of becoming invasive.
**'Painter's Palette'** has variegated leaves,
marked with yellow, creamy white, pink,
red and various shades of green.

*P. virginiana* 'Painter's Palette' (above)
*P. polymorpha* (below)

P. polymorpha *is a favorite with landscape
designers partly because it is used frequently
by the world-renowned designer, Wolfgang
Oehme of Oehme & VanSweden.*

---

**Also called:** fleeceflower, knotweed
**Features:** creamy white, pink and red summer
to fall flowers; low maintenance; attractive
foliage; habit **Height:** 6–48"
**Spread:** 12–36" **Hardiness:** zones 5–8

# Phlox
*Phlox*

Phlox comprises a widely diverse group of beautiful plants for sun to partial shade.

## Growing
Garden phlox and early phlox prefers **full sun**. Moss phlox and woodland phlox prefers **partial shade**. Creeping phlox prefers **light to partial shade** but tolerates heavy shade. All like **fertile, humus-rich, moist, well-drained** soil. Divide after flowering.

Do not prune creeping phlox in fall—it will already be forming next spring's flowers.

## Tips
Low-growing species are useful in a rock garden or at the front of a border. Taller species may be used in the middle of a border, particularly when planted in groups.

Garden phlox requires good air circulation to help prevent mildew. Thin out large stands to help keep the air flowing. Early phlox is more mildew-resistant. Deadhead after blooming.

## Recommended
*P. divaricata* (blue phlox, wild sweet William, woodland phlox) is a spreading, semi-evergreen perennial with lavender blue to pale purple and white flowers with notched tips. A wide variety of cultivars are available with white, purple-blue and pink flowers, along with variable forms.

*P. maculata* (Maculata Group; early phlox, wild sweet William) forms an upright clump of hairy stems and pink, purple or white flowers.

P. *subulata* (above), P. *paniculata* (below)

*P. paniculata* (Paniculata Group; garden phlox) blooms in summer and fall. It has many cultivars in a variety of sizes and flower colors.

*P. stolonifera* (creeping phlox) is a low, spreading plant with purple or pink flowers. It grows roots where the stems touch the ground.

*P. subulata* (moss phlox, creeping phlox, moss pinks) is very low growing.

Features: white, orange, red, blue, purple, pink, spring, summer or fall flowers; plant habit Height: 2"–4' Spread: 12–36" Hardiness: zones 3–8

# Russian Sage
*Perovskia*

*P. atriplicifolia* (above), *P. atriplicifolia* 'Filigran' (below)

The silvery foliage of Russian sage topped with wands of tiny, bluish flowers provides contrast to other summer bloomers, and it is sure to catch your attention no matter where it is placed. Its fragrance is an added bonus.

### Growing

Russian sage prefers **full sun**. The soil should be **poor to moderately fertile** and **well drained**. Too much water and nitrogen will cause this plant's growth to flop, so do not plant it next to heavy feeders. Russian sage cannot be divided.

*Russian sage is rarely troubled by pests or diseases.*

In spring, when new growth appears low on the branches, or in fall, cut the plant back hard to about 6–12" to encourage vigorous, bushy growth.

### Tips

The silvery foliage and blue flowers work well with other plants in the back of a mixed border and soften the appearance of daylilies. Russian sage can also create a soft screen in a natural garden or on a dry bank.

### Recommended

*P. atriplicifolia* is a loose, upright plant with silvery white, finely divided foliage. The small, lavender blue flowers are loosely held on silvery, branched stems. Cultivars are available.

*P.* 'Blue Spire' is an upright plant with deep blue flowers and feathery leaves.

---

**Features:** blue to purple mid-summer to fall flowers; attractive habit; fragrant, gray-green foliage **Height:** 2–4' **Spread:** 3–4' **Hardiness:** zones 4–9

# Sedum
*Sedum*

Some gardeners aren't aware of just how useful this diverse family of plants is. Sedums feature outstanding foliage that complements surrounding plants throughout the season.

## Growing
Sedums prefer **full sun** or **partial shade**. The soil should be of **average fertility**, and **very well drained**. Divide in spring when needed.

## Tips
Low-growing sedums make wonderful groundcovers and additions to rock gardens or rock walls. They edge beds and borders beautifully. Taller sedums give a lovely late-season display in a bed or border.

## Recommended
There are 300 to 500 species of sedum throughout the Northern Hemisphere, including the following popular selections.

*S. acre* (gold moss stonecrop) is a low-growing, wide-spreading plant that bears small, yellow-green flowers.

*S.* '**Autumn Joy**' (*Hylotelephium* 'Autumn Joy'; autumn joy sedum) is an upright hybrid with flowers that open pink or red and later fade to deep bronze.

*S. spectabile* (showy stonecrop) is an upright species with pink flowers. Cultivars are available.

*S. spurium* (two-row stonecrop) forms a low, wide mat of foliage with deep pink or white flowers. Cultivars, including '**Dragon's Blood**,' bear colorful foliage.

S. *acre* (above), S. 'Autumn Joy' (below)

*'Autumn Joy' brings color to the late-season garden, when few flowers are in bloom.*

Also called: stonecrop  Features: yellow, white, red, pink summer to fall flowers; decorative, fleshy foliage; easy to grow
Height: 2–30"  Spread: 12" to indefinite
Hardiness: zones 3–9

# Shasta Daisy
*Leucanthemum*

Shasta daisy is one of the most popular perennials because it is easy to grow and the blooms are bright and plentiful and work well as cut flowers.

### Growing
Shasta daisy grows well in **full sun** or **partial shade**. The soil should be **fertile, moist** and **well drained**. Pinch plants back in spring to encourage compact, bushy growth. Divide every year or two in spring to maintain plant vigor. Fall-planted shasta daisy may not become established in time to survive winter. Plants can be short-lived in zone 5.

Deadheading extends the bloom by several weeks. Start seeds indoors in spring or direct sow into warm soil.

### Tips
Use shasta daisy as a single plant or massed in groups. Shorter varieties can be used in many garden settings, and taller varieties may need support if exposed to windy situations. The flowers can be cut for fresh arrangements.

### Recommended
*L.* x *superbum* forms a large clump of dark green leaves and stems. It bears white, daisy flowers with yellow centers all summer, often until first frost. 'Becky' has strong, wind-resistant stems, with blooms lasting up to eight weeks. 'Crazy Daisy' is a tall cultivar with frilled double flowers ideal for cutting.

L. x superbum (above & below)

**Features:** white early-summer to fall flowers with yellow centers  **Height:** 1–4'
**Spread:** 15–24"  **Hardiness:** zones 4–9

# Wandflower

### *Gaura*

The pink and white flowers floating high above wandflower's tall, slender stems resemble butterflies whirling in the sunlight.

## Growing

Wandflower prefers **full sun**. The soil should be **fertile, moist** and **well drained**. A deep taproot helps established plants tolerate drought but makes division difficult.

Deadheading wandflower will keep it flowering right up until the end of the season, help prevent excessive self-seeding and keep the plant tidy.

## Tips

Wandflower makes a good addition for borders. Its color and appearance have a softening effect on brighter flowers. Although it bears only a few flowers at a time, it blooms for the entire summer. It is most effective when used en masse or with large, bold plants in the background.

## Recommended

*G. lindheimeri* is a clump-forming plant. It bears clusters of star-shaped, white flowers from pink buds. The flowers fade back to pink with age. **'Siskiyou Pink'** is a shorter variety, with bright pink flowers and foliage that is marked with reddish purple. **'Whirling Butterflies'** grows up to 36" tall and tends to have more flowers in bloom at a time.

*There are about 20 species of wandflower, and they are all native to North America.*

G. *lindheimeri* 'Whirling Butterflies' (above)
G. *lindheimeri* (below)

---

**Features:** delicate pink and white flowers; scarlet stems in winter; decorative habit
**Height:** 6"–4' **Spread:** 24–36"
**Hardiness:** zones 5–9

# Wormwood

## *Artemisia*

A. *stelleriana* 'Silver Brocade' (above)
A. *ludoviciana* 'Valerie Finnis' (below)

The silvery foliage of wormwood provides wonderful contrast and texture to the perennial border year-round.

### Growing

Wormwood grows best in **full sun**. The soil should be of **average to high fertility** and **well drained**. It dislikes wet, humid conditions.

Wormwoods respond well to pruning in late spring. If you prune before May, frost may kill any new growth. When plants look straggly, cut them back hard to encourage new growth and to maintain a neater form. Divide them every year or two when the plants thin out in their centers.

### Tips

Use wormwoods in rock gardens and borders. Their silvery gray or pale green foliage makes them good backdrop plants to use behind brightly colored flowers, or to fill in spaces between other plants. Wormwoods also add color to the winter landscape. Smaller forms may be used to create knot gardens.

### Recommended

A. *ludoviciana* (white sage, silver sage) cultivars are upright, clump-forming plants with silvery white foliage.

A. *schmidtiana* (silvermound artemisia) is a low, dense, mound-forming perennial with feathery, hairy, silvery gray foliage. 'Nana' grows only half the size of the species.

A. *stelleriana* 'Silver Brocade' is a low, somewhat spreading cultivar with soft, pale gray leaves.

*The genus name may honor either Artemisia, a botanist and medical researcher from 353 BC and the sister of King Mausolus, or Artemis, goddess of the hunt and the moon in Greek mythology.*

**Also called:** sage **Features:** silvery gray, green feathery or deeply lobed foliage **Height:** 6"–6' **Spread:** 6–36" **Hardiness:** zones 3–8

# Yarrow

*Achillea*

Yarrows are informal, tough plants with a fantastic color range.

## Growing

Grow yarrows in **full sun** in **well-drained** soil of **average fertility** but avoid heavy clay. Yarrows tolerate drought and poor soil, but do not thrive in heavy, wet soil or very humid conditions. Excessively rich soil or too much nitrogen results in weak, floppy growth.

Divide every three to four years in spring to maintain plant vigor. Deadhead to prolong blooming. Once the flowerheads begin to fade, cut them back to the lateral buds. Basal foliage should be left in place over the winter and tidied up in spring.

## Tips

Cottage gardens, wildflower gardens and mixed borders are perfect places for these informal plants. They thrive in hot, dry locations where nothing else will grow.

## Recommended

Many yarrow species, cultivars and hybrids are available.

**A. *filipendulina*** forms a clump of fern-like foliage and bears yellow flowers. It has been used to develop several hybrids and cultivars.

**A. *millefolium*** (common yarrow) forms a clump of soft, finely divided foliage and bears white flowers. Many cultivars exist with flowers in a wide range of colors.

*A. millefolium* 'Paprika' (above), *A. filipendulina* (below)

*Yarrows make excellent groundcovers. They send up shoots and flowers from a low basal point and may be mowed periodically without excessive damage to the plant. Mower blades should be kept at least 4" high.*

---

**Features:** white, yellow, red, orange, pink, purple mid-summer to early-fall flowers; attractive foliage; spreading habit **Height:** 6"–3'
**Spread:** 12–36" **Hardiness:** zones 3–9

# Yucca

*Yucca*

Y. filamentosa 'Golden Sword' (above)
Y. filamentosa (below)

Planted alone or en masse, yucca makes a strong architectural statement all year.

## Growing

Yucca grows best in **full sun,** in **light, sandy, well-drained, neutral to slightly acidic** soil, but it adapts to most well-drained soils.

Pruning is not needed, but the flower spikes can be removed when flowering is finished, and dead leaves can be removed as needed.

## Tips

Yucca looks great as an accent plant in beds, borders and foundation plantings. It also looks good as a specimen in pots, planters and urns. The variegated varieties add color and texture to beds and borders.

## Recommended

**Y. filamentosa** is a clump-forming shrub that is sometimes grown as a perennial. It produces a stemless rosette of lance-shaped, stiff, dark green leaves with razor sharp edges. Nodding, bell-shaped flowers are borne on upright spikes in mid- to late summer. A variety of cultivars are available with variegated leaves, including **'Bright Edge'** and **'Golden Sword.'** **'Hofer's Blue'** has bluish green foliage.

*The striking white flowers are edible raw or cooked—they taste like Belgian endive. Try adding them to a salad.*

**Also called:** Adam's needle
**Features:** rounded rosette of long, stiff, spiky, evergreen leaves; white summer flowers; striking foliage; appealing habit
**Height:** 16"–4'; up to 6' when in flower
**Spread:** 5' **Hardiness:** zones 4–10

# Arborvitae
*Thuja*

*T. occidentalis* 'Sherwood Moss' (above), *T. occidentalis* (below)

Arborvitaes are found throughout Kansas because of their durability, good looks, adaptation to a variety of conditions, range of shapes and, perhaps most importantly, soft needles.

## Growing

Most arborvitae selections prefer **full sun,** but there are a few that tolerate shade. The soil should be of **average fertility, moist** and **well drained**. These plants enjoy humidity and are often found growing near marshy areas. Arborvitae performs best with some shelter from wind, especially in winter, when the foliage can dry out and give the plant a rather brown, drab appearance.

## Tips

Large varieties of arborvitae make excellent specimen trees; smaller cultivars can be used in foundation plantings and shrub borders, and as formal or informal hedges.

## Recommended

*T. occidentalis* (eastern arborvitae, eastern white cedar) is a narrow, pyramidal tree with scale-like needles. A wide variety of cultivars are available in dwarf forms, variable shades of yellow and green and overall varied habits including narrow and globe forms.

---

**Also called:** cedar **Features:** small to large evergreen shrub or tree; foliage; bark; form
**Height:** 18"–50' **Spread:** 18"–15'
**Hardiness:** zones 2–7

# Barberry
*Berberis*

B. thunbergii 'Aurea' (above), B. thunbergii 'Atropurpurea' (below)

Barberries add bold contrast in a shrub border, but it's best to put them in the center of the planting. Effective placement will maximize their visual interest while preventing the decidedly unpleasant experience of walking into them.

## Growing

Barberry develops the best fall color when grown in **full sun,** but it tolerates partial shade. Any **well-drained** soil is suitable. This plant tolerates drought and urban conditions but suffers in poorly drained, wet soil.

## Tips

Large barberry plants make great hedges with formidable prickles. They can be very effective for discouraging foot (or dog) traffic from cutting through your yard. Barberry can also be included in shrub and mixed borders. Small cultivars can be grown in rock gardens, in raised beds and along rock walls.

## Recommended

*B.* x *gladwynensis* '**William Penn**' is a mound-forming evergreen shrub with a dense habit. It has arching branches and dark, lush foliage that turns bronze in winter. Yellow flowers are produced in spring, followed by purple-yellow fruit. It will reach 3–4' in height and 4–5' spread.

*B. thunbergii* (Japanese barberry) is a dense shrub with a broad, rounded habit. The foliage is bright green and turns shades of orange, red or purple in fall. Yellow spring flowers are followed by glossy red fruit later in summer. Many cultivars have been developed for their variable foliage color, including shades of purple, yellow and variegated varieties.

**Features:** prickly, deciduous shrub; foliage; flowers; fruit **Height:** 2–6' **Spread:** 18"–6' **Hardiness:** zones 4–8

# Beautyberry
## *Callicarpa*

*C. dichotoma* 'Early Amethyst' (below)

This florists' favorite adds pizzazz to your fall garden.

## Growing
Beautyberry grows well in **full sun** or **light shade**. The soil should be of **average fertility** and **well drained**. Since it flowers and fruits on new wood, cut the entire shrub back in late winter for best results.

## Tips
Beautyberries can be used in natural settings and in shrub and mixed borders, where the uniquely colored fruit will add interest and contrast. The colorful fruit-covered branches are often cut for fresh or dried arrangements.

## Recommended
*C. dichotoma* (purple beautyberry) is a dense, upright shrub with bright green foliage. It bears pale pink flowers, followed by bright purple fruit. This species grows 4' tall and wide. Cultivars are available with white fruit. **'Early Amethyst'** produces an abundance of purple berries.

*Planting beautyberry in groups will ensure heavy fruit production.*

**Features:** bushy, deciduous shrub; arching stems that bear purple late-summer or fall fruit **Height:** 3–10' **Spread:** 3–6' **Hardiness:** zones 5–10

# Beautybush

*Kolkwitzia*

*K. amabilis* (above & below)

Beautybush has a bold winter outline and is a nice contrast to other deciduous shrubs as well as evergreens year-round. It also offers a solid pink bouquet of blossoms in late spring to early summer for 10–14 days.

### Growing

Beautybush flowers most profusely in **full sun.** The soil should be **fertile** and **well drained.** It adapts to a variety of conditions and is drought tolerant. Prune out one-third of the old wood each year after flowering. Old, overgrown plants can be cut right back to the ground if they need rejuvenation.

### Tips

Beautybush can be included in a shrub border. It can also be grown as a specimen shrub, but it isn't exceptionally attractive when not in flower.

### Recommended

*K. amabilis* is a large shrub with arching canes. Clusters of bell-shaped flowers in many shades of pink are borne in late spring or early summer. **'Pink Cloud'** is a popular cultivar with vivid pink flowers. It is not quite as cold hardy as the species. **'Rosea'** produces deep pink flowers.

*The name* Kolkwitzia *honors Richard Kolkwitz, a German professor of botany;* amabilis *is Latin for 'lovely.'*

**Features:** suckering, deciduous, arching shrub; late-spring flowers **Height:** 6–15' **Spread:** 5–11' **Hardiness:** zones 4–8

# Chokecherry
### *Prunus*

*P. virginiana* 'Schubert'

Chokecherries are so beautiful and uplifting after the gray days of winter that few gardeners can resist them.

## Growing

These flowering trees prefer **full sun.** The soil should be of **average fertility, moist** and **well drained.** Shallow roots will emerge if the tree is not getting sufficient water.

## Tips

Chokecherries are beautiful as specimen trees and are small enough for almost any garden. They're often best planted in areas that need a boost of color. The cultivars' foliage emerges in a lush shade of green but changes to a deep, red wine color for the rest of the growing season.

## Recommended

*P. virginiana* is a conical tree or shrub that has a tendency to sucker. This deciduous species has a broad growth habit with glossy, medium to dark green foliage. It bears small white flowers in late spring, followed by tiny red to dark purple, round berries. It grows 25–30' tall and wide. **'Schubert'** ('Canada Red') is the more popular selection. This cultivar bears green leaves early in spring but later the foliage changes to a deep, dark, red wine color and remains so until fall. The flowers are borne with a hint of pink, followed by black berries. The cultivar is also slightly smaller in size and more elliptical in form.

*Birds and butterflies are fond of its flowers, foliage and fruit.*

**Features:** upright, rounded, deciduous tree or shrub; spring to early-summer flowers; fruit
**Height:** 20–30' **Spread:** 20–35'
**Hardiness:** zones 3–8

# Coralberry
## *Symphoricarpos*

Although certain species of coralberry are native to parts of Kansas, people often think of them being harnessed and put to work in the city, where their suckering roots bind soil on hillsides and where their quick-growing, shrubby forms make adaptable screens.

### Growing

Coralberries grow well in **full sun, partial** or **light shade** in any soil that is **fertile and well drained**. These plants can withstand pollution, drought and exposure.

### Tips

Use in shrub or mixed borders, in woodland gardens or as screens or informal hedges. The berries offer an interesting element in the fall and winter months.

Coralberries are known to spread by suckers, but they can be controlled by mowing or trimming the suckers down.

### Recommended

*S. albus* (common snowberry) is a rounded, suckering shrub with arching branches, small, delicate pinkish white flowers and white berries. It tolerates clay soil.

*S.* x *chenaultii* (Indian currant, Chenault coralberry) is an erect, well-branched shrub that spreads by suckers. It bears greenish white flowers and pink-tinged or pink-spotted, white fruit. Cultivars are available in low, spreading forms.

*S.* x *doorenbosii* AMETHYST ('Kordes,' amethyst coralberry) bears deep purplish pink fruit from late summer into fall and grows 3–5' tall.

*S. albus* (above & below)

*The berries are not edible and should be left for the birds.*

---

**Also called:** snowberry, buckbrush
**Features:** rounded or spreading deciduous shrub; dark green foliage; fall and winter fruit; white or white tinged with pink, green, yellow summer flowers
**Height:** 2–6' **Spread:** 3–12' **Hardiness:** zones 3–7

# Cotoneaster

*Cotoneaster*

C. *horizontalis* (left), C. *apiculatus* (above)

Cotoneasters come in many shapes and sizes, the most remarkable being the groundcover species that spill into layers of pendulous branches. All cotoneasters have multi-season interest—abundant spring flowers, summer fruit formation and charming orangy red fall color.

## Growing

Cotoneasters grow well in **full sun** or **partial shade**. The soil should be of **average fertility** and **well drained**.

## Tips

Cotoneasters can be included in shrub or mixed borders. Low spreaders work well as groundcover and shrubby species can be used to form hedges. Larger species are grown as small specimen trees and some low-growers are grafted onto standards and grown as small, weeping trees.

## Recommended

There are many cotoneasters to choose from including *C. apiculatus* (cranberry cotoneaster), a wide-spreading, low, shrubby plant similar to *C. horizontalis* (rockspray cotoneaster), which is a distinctive species with an attractive herringbone branching pattern. It grows 2–3' in height and 5–8' in spread. Light pink flowers are produced in early summer, followed by red fruit in fall. The leaves turn bright red in fall. *C. lucidus* (hedge cotoneaster) is an upright, rounded evergreen shrub with spreading branches and shiny dark green leaves that turn crimson red in the fall. Tiny pinkish white flowers are produced in early spring, followed by dark berries. This species is most commonly used for hedging, planted in rows and sheared for a formal appearance.

**Features:** evergreen or deciduous shrubs; foliage; early-summer flowers; persistent fruit; variety of forms **Height:** 6"–6' **Spread:** 2–8' **Hardiness:** zones 3–8

*Although cotoneaster berries are not poisonous, they can cause stomach upset if eaten in large quantities. The foliage may be toxic.*

# Crabapple
*Malus*

For winter-sapped Kansasans, there are few trees that present as magnificent a display of spring flowers as a crabapple tree in full bloom.

### Growing

Crabapples prefer **full sun** but tolerate partial shade. The soil should be of **average to rich fertility, moist** and **well drained**. These trees tolerate damp soil.

### Tips

Crabapples make excellent specimen plants. Many varieties are quite small, so there is one to suit almost any size of garden.

### Recommended

There are hundreds of crabapples available, some of which are grown strictly for their fruit while others are grown for their ornamental value. When choosing a species, variety or cultivar, one of the most important attributes to look for is disease resistance. Even the most beautiful plant will never look good if ravaged by pests or disease. Flower color includes white, pink, and even red, and the fruit, which birds love, can be yellow, orange or red. The foliage is often green, but one of the most distinguishing features of most ornamental selections is the degree of burgundy in the foliage and pink in the flowers. There are columnar and weeping forms as well as vase-shaped to spreading selections. The following cultivars and hybrids are some of the more popular selections available throughout the state including **'Donald Wyman,' 'Golden Raindrops,' 'Prairifire'** and **'Red Jade.'** *M. sargentii* is a spreading shrub or small tree with dark green foliage and abundant white flowers followed by dark red fruit.

---

**Features:** rounded, upright, mounded or spreading, small to medium, deciduous tree; spring flowers; late-season and winter fruit; fall foliage; habit; bark **Height:** 5–30' **Spread:** 6–30' **Hardiness:** zones 4–8

# Dogwood
*Cornus*

C. *alba* cultivar (above), C. *alba* (below)

While the flowering dogwood tree is difficult to grow on the Kansas prairie, the tougher dogwood shrubs, with their wintertime red or yellow stems, thrive and spread throughout the state.

## Growing

Dogwoods prefer **full sun** or **partial shade**, with the best stem colors developing in full sun. The soil should be of **average to high fertility, high in organic matter, neutral** or **slightly acidic, well drained** and **moist**.

To maintain the vivid stem color, remove one third of the oldest, discolored branches all the way back to the ground every three years to encourage new growth and more vivid stem color.

## Tips

Use dogwoods in a shrub or mixed border. They look best planted in groups.

**Features:** deciduous shrub; late-spring to early-summer flowers; fall and winter stem and foliage color; fruit; habit **Height:** 3–10' **Spread:** 3–10' **Hardiness:** zones 2–7

## Recommended

*C. alba* (Tatarian dogwood) is a shrub with green stems that turn bright red as winter approaches. The species can grow 10' tall and wide. Many cultivars are available including **'Argenteo-marginata,'** which bears creamy white and green variegated foliage.

*C. sericea* (red-osier, red-twig dogwood) is a fast-growing shrub that also has bright red stems. Improved selections include **'Bailey,'** which produces rich green foliage that turns reddish purple in the fall, and **'Flaviramea'** (yellow-twig dogwood) that features bright yellow stems. It grows 4' tall and wide.

*C. stolonifera* **'Farrow'** ('Arctic Fire') is more compact than the species, growing only 3–4' and does not sucker.

# Elderberry

*Sambucus*

S. nigra 'Gerda' (above), S. racemosa (below)

Elderberries have what we all want in a shrub—flowers (often fragrant), berries and interesting foliage. New selections with finely cut, purple-black leaves, similar to those of Japanese maples, have made the elderberry a popular choice with gardeners.

## Growing

Elderberries grow well in **full sun** or **partial shade** in **moist, well-drained** soil of **average fertility**. Cultivars with burgundy or black leaf color develop the best color in full sun, whereas cultivars with yellow leaf color develop the best color in light or partial shade. These plants tolerate dry soil once established. Most elderberries should be cut back to the ground in fall or early spring to stay tidy.

## Tips

Elderberries can be used in a shrub or mixed border, in a natural woodland garden or next to a pond or other water feature. Plants with interesting or colorful foliage can be used as specimen plants or focal points in the garden.

## Recommended

*S. nigra* (European elderberry, black elderberry) is an upright, bushy shrub with mid-green foliage and musky scented, creamy white flower clusters. The flowers are followed by spherical, glossy black fruit in mid- to late summer. Several cultivars are available including **'Black Beauty'** and **'Black Lace,'** bearing dark purplish brown to black, deeply cut, ornate foliage, and **'Madonna,'** which produces creamy white and yellow variegated foliage.

**Features:** large, bushy, deciduous shrub; early-summer flowers; fruit; foliage
**Height:** 3–8'  **Spread:** 3–8'
**Hardiness:** zones 3–9

# Elm

*Ulmus*

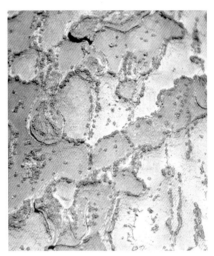

*U. parvifolia* (both photos)

Elms are known as the classic street tree throughout the United States, including Kansas; they create grand archways along many urban and suburban streets. In recent years, Dutch elm disease has dealt a devastating blow to our elms. Fortunately, resistant selections are available on the market, along with watchdog groups to control the spread and ultimate devastation of our beloved elms.

## Growing

Elms grow well in **full sun** or **partial shade**. They adapt to most soil types and conditions but prefer a **moist, fertile soil**. Elms are tolerant of urban conditions, including salt from roadways.

## Tips

Elms are attractive where they have plenty of room to grow on large properties and in parks. Smaller species and cultivars make attractive specimen and shade trees.

**Features:** variable, rounded to vase-shaped, deciduous tree; habit; fall color; bark
**Height:** 40–60' **Spread:** 35–50'
**Hardiness:** zones 5–9

## Recommended

*U. parvifolia* (lacebark elm, Chinese elm) is an upright, spreading, deciduous tree with a rounded habit. It produces showy flaking bark and pendent shoots, clothed in leathery dark green foliage that can turn red or yellow in fall. Tiny red flowers may be borne in late summer followed by winged green fruit, but only if the growing season is long enough. This species can reach 60' in height and 35–50' in width. Many cultivars are available including ATHENA, ALLEE and 'Emerald Prairie,' the cultivar with the highest resistance to leaf spot that was developed in Wichita by John Pair.

# Filbert

*Corylus*

C. avellana 'Contorta' (above & below)

This underused woody ornamental deserves more attention, most notably the novelty cultivar 'Contorta.' Use this cultivar as a specimen plant in a prominent area where its twisted stems and foliage can be fully appreciated.

## Growing

Filberts grow equally well in **full sun** or **partial shade.** The soil should be **fertile** and **well drained.**

These plants require very little pruning but tolerate it well. Entire plants can be cut back to within 6" of the ground to encourage new growth in spring. On grafted specimens of corkscrew hazel, suckers that come up from the roots should be cut out. They will be easy to spot because they won't have the twisted habit.

## Tips

Use filberts as specimens or in shrub or mixed borders.

## Recommended

*C. avellana* (European hazelnut, European filbert) grows as a large shrub or small tree. Male plants bear long, dangling catkins in late winter and early spring, and female plants develop edible nuts. Cultivars are more commonly grown than the species. **'Contorta'** (contorted filbert, corkscrew hazel, Harry Lauder's walking stick) is perhaps the best-known cultivar. It grows 8–10' tall. The stems, branches and leaves are twisted and contorted. This is a particularly interesting feature in winter when the bare stems are most visible. Cut out any growth that is not twisted. An excellent specimen plant.

---

**Also called:** hazelnut **Features:** early-spring catkins; nuts; foliage; large, dense, deciduous shrub or small tree **Height:** 8–10'
**Spread:** 8–10' **Hardiness:** zones 3–9

# Forsythia

*Forsythia*

Many people have a similar attitude to Forsythia that they do to visiting relatives—it's fabulous to see them when they burst into bloom after a long, dreary winter, but they just seem to be taking up garden space once they are done flowering. However, new selections with more decorative foliage have made them more appealing.

## Growing

Forsythias grow best in **full sun** but some varieties tolerate or prefer **light** or **partial shade.** The soil should be of **average fertility, moist** and **well drained**. These plants are more cold hardy than their flower buds.

## Tips

Include forsythias in a shrub or mixed border where other flowering plants will provide interest once the forsythias' early-season glory has passed.

## Recommended

*F.* x *intermedia* is a large shrub with upright stems that arch as they mature. It grows 5–10' tall and spreads 5–12'. Bright yellow flowers emerge before the leaves in early to mid-spring. Many cultivars are available.

*F.* x *intermedia* (above & below)

*Forsythias can be used as hedging plants, but they look most attractive and flower best when left unsheared and grown informally.*

**Features:** spreading, deciduous shrub with upright or arching branches; attractive, early to mid-spring yellow flowers **Height:** 2–10' **Spread:** 3–15' **Hardiness:** zones 3–8

# Golden-Rain Tree
*Koelreuteria*

*K. paniculata* (above & below)

Golden-rain tree is one of the few trees with yellow flowers and one of the only trees to flower in mid-summer.

### Growing
Golden-rain tree grows best in **full sun**. The soil should be **average to fertile, moist** and **well drained**. This tree can tolerate heat, drought, wind and air pollution. It also adapts to most pH levels and different soil types.

### Tips
Golden-rain tree is an excellent shade or specimen tree for small properties. It adapts to a wide range of soils, making it useful in many gardens. The fruit is not messy and won't stain a patio or deck if planted to shade these areas.

### Recommended
*K. paniculata* is a rounded, spreading tree, 30–40' tall and wide. It bears long clusters of small, yellow flowers in mid-summer, followed by red-tinged, green capsular fruit that resemble little Chinese lanterns. The leaves are somewhat lacy in appearance. The foliage may turn bright yellow in fall. **'Fastigiata'** is an upright, columnar tree that reaches 25' in height, with a spread of no more than 6'.

---

**Features:** fast-growing, rounded, spreading, deciduous tree; attractive foliage; unique fruit; mid-summer flowers **Height:** 25–40' **Spread:** 6–40' **Hardiness:** zones 5–8

# Hackberry
*Celtis*

ackberry, with its grace and strength, can tolerate all weather conditions in Kansas.

## Growing
Hackberry prefers **full sun to partial shade**. It adapts to a variety of soil types including poor and dry soils. **Deep soils** with **adequate moisture** and **drainage** are best.

## Tips
Hackberry is an ideal shade tree specimen for expansive, windy areas. It requires lots of space to reach its full size.

## Recommended
*C. occidentalis* is a large spreading tree with an upright vase shape. The head is made up of arching branches covered in simple but classic foliage. Inconspicuous flowers emerge in spring followed by edible fruit that ripens from yellow or red-orange to purple in fall. The bark gets corky as the tree matures.

*Hackberry has everything to offer but asks little in return. It will provide beautiful fall color and cool shade in the hot summer months. Hackberry also attracts wildlife.*

C. occidentalis (above & below)

---

**Also called:** American hackberry, common hackberry, nettle tree **Features:** high-headed, oval, decidudous tree; hardiness; colorful berries; tolerance to poor conditions
**Height:** 40–60' **Spread:** 30–50'
**Hardiness:** zones 2–8

# Hydrangea
*Hydrangea*

*H. quercifolia* (above), *H. macrophylla* cultivars (below)

uge blooms and an extended blooming period are two reasons gardeners have pushed these old-time favorites back into the limelight.

## Growing

Hydrangeas grow best in **partial sun** with afternoon shade. *H. arborescens* tolerates heavy shade. *H. paniculata* tolerates sun. Shade or partial shade reduces leaf and flower scorch in hotter regions. The soil should be of **average to high fertility, humus rich, moist** and **well drained**. These plants perform best in cool, moist conditions.

## Tips

Hydrangeas come in many forms and have many landscape uses. They can be included in shrub or mixed borders, used as specimens or informal barriers and planted in groups or containers. While most hydrangeas are grown for their extravagant flowers, the oakleaf hydrangea is grown for its unique foliage.

## Recommended

*H. arborescens* (smooth hydrangea) is a rounded shrub that flowers well in shade. Its cultivars bear large clusters of showy, white blossoms.

*H. macrophylla* (bigleaf hydrangea, mophead hydrangea) is a rounded or mounding shrub that bears pink or blue flowers from mid- to late summer. Newer, hardier, longer-blooming selections are available including **'Endless Summer.'**

*H. paniculata* (panicle hydrangea) is a spreading to upright large shrub or small tree that bears white flowers. **'Grandiflora'** (Peegee hydrangea) is a commonly available cultivar. **'Little Lamb'** is a smaller cultivar.

*H. quercifolia* (oakleaf hydrangea) is a mound-forming shrub with attractive, exfoliating bark, large, oak-like leaves that turn bronze to bright red in fall and conical clusters of sterile and fertile flowers.

*H. serrata* (lacecap hydrangea) is a compact, deciduous shrub with narrow leaves and flattened flower clusters in pink and blue. The cultivars are more popular than the species and often bloom for longer periods.

---

**Features:** deciduous; mounding or spreading shrub or tree; flowers; habit; foliage; bark
**Height:** 3–25' **Spread:** 3–20'
**Hardiness:** zones 3–8

# Japanese Pagoda
*Sophora*

*S. japonica* (above & below)

If you are looking for an undemanding, stately tree for the garden and have the space, consider the Japanese pagoda. It will reach a grand size and cast a light shade, so turf grass and other groundcovers can grow beneath it.

## Growing

Japanese pagoda grows best in **full sun.** The soil should be of **average fertility** and **well drained.** Once established, this species tolerates most conditions, even polluted urban settings. Pruning is rarely required.

## Tips

Use Japanese pagoda as a specimen tree or a shade tree. The cultivar 'Pendula' can be used in borders.

Plant in a sheltered location to provide protection to young trees, which can be quite tender until they are established.

**Features:** dense, rounded, wide-spreading, deciduous tree; fall foliage; fragrant summer flowers **Height:** 10–75' **Spread:** 10–50' **Hardiness:** zones: 4–7

The seeds are poisonous and can even be fatal if eaten.

## Recommended

*S. japonica* may reach heights of 100' in the wild, but it usually grows to about 50' in garden settings. It grows quickly to about 20', and then the pace of growth becomes slower. It bears fragrant white flowers in summer, and the foliage may turn yellow in fall. **'Pendula'** has long, drooping branches that are usually grafted to a standard, creating a small, dramatic weeping tree. The size depends on the height of the standard, usually 10–25' tall, with an equal or greater spread. This cultivar rarely flowers.

# Juniper
*Juniperus*

*J. horizontalis* 'Blue Chip' (above)
*J. horizontalis* 'Blue Prince' (below)

ew shrubs are as admired as junipers for their hardiness, adaptability to soil and light conditions, year-round color and tolerance of pruning. There is a juniper with the right form, color and texture available for just about any landscaping situation.

## Growing
Junipers prefer **full sun** but tolerate light shade. The soil should be of **average fertility** and **well drained**, but junipers tolerate most conditions.

## Tips
Junipers make prickly barriers, hedges and windbreaks. They can be used in borders, as specimens or in groups. The low-growing species can be used in rock gardens and as groundcover. For interesting evergreen color, mix the yellow-foliaged junipers with the blue-needled varieties.

## Recommended
Junipers vary from species to species and often from cultivar to cultivar within a species. *J. chinensis* (Chinese juniper) is a conical tree or spreading shrub that is similar to the native Eastern red cedar but is resistant to cedar apple rust. *J. communis* (common juniper) is a spreading shrub to a columnar tree. *J. horizontalis* (creeping juniper) is a prostrate, creeping groundcover. *J. sabina* (savin juniper) is a spreading to erect shrub. *J. scopulorum* (Rocky Mountain juniper) can be upright, rounded, weeping or spreading. *J. squamata* (singleseed juniper) forms a prostrate or low, spreading shrub or a small, upright tree. *J. virginiana* (eastern redcedar) is a durable, upright or wide-spreading tree often used in windbreaks.

**Features:** conical or columnar tree, rounded or spreading shrub, prostrate groundcover; evergreen; foliage; variety of color, size and habit **Height:** 4"–70' **Spread:** 1–48' **Hardiness:** zones 3–8

# Kentucky Coffee Tree

*Gymnocladus*

This splendid specimen is finally receiving the attention it deserves, and it should be given serious consideration when choosing a large shade tree. It matures into an elegant, billowy, feathered cloud of beauty that will be much admired for years to come.

## Growing

Kentucky coffee tree grows best in **full sun**. It prefers **fertile, moist, well-drained** soil but adapts to a range of conditions, tolerating alkaline soil, drought and urban situations. Kentucky coffee tree is one of the last trees to leaf out in spring.

## Tips

Ideal for spacious landscapes, parks and golf courses, Kentucky coffee tree makes an attractive specimen tree.

## Recommended

*G. dioica* has striking bluish green foliage with rich yellow fall color and bears large clusters of white flowers. The ridged bark adds interest to the winter landscape. A wide variety of cultivars are available.

*G. dioica* (above & below)

*Kentucky coffee tree rarely suffers from pest or disease problems.*

**Features:** upright to spreading, deciduous tree; summer and fall foliage; fruit; bark  **Height:** 50–60'
**Spread:** 30–45'
**Hardiness:** zones 3–8

# Lilac
*Syringa*

S. reticulata 'Ivory Silk' (above), S. meyeri (below)

Lilacs are easy to take for granted during most of the year, except for the days in spring when they're in heavenly fragrant bloom.

### Growing
Lilacs grow best in **full sun**. The soil should be **fertile, humus rich** and **well drained**. These plants tolerate open, windy locations.

### Tips
Include lilacs in a shrub or mixed border or use them to create an informal hedge. Japanese tree lilac can be used as a specimen tree.

### Recommended
The following is a short list of really reliable selections including some of the newer cultivars that tend to be smaller than older lilac species. Buy one in bloom if fragrance is important to you.

**S. x *chinensis*** (Chinese lilac, Rouen lilac) is a bushy shrub with arching to spreading branches. It bears purple flowers in late spring and grows 15' tall and wide.

**S. *meyeri*** (dwarf Korean lilac) is a compact, rounded shrub that grows 3–5' tall and 3–7' wide. It produces fragrant pink or lavender flowers in late spring and early summer. It does not sucker profusely. Cultivars are available.

**S. *reticulata*** (Japanese tree lilac) is an oval to rounded large shrub or small tree that bears white flowers. It is very hardy and suitable for planting under power lines. Improved cultivars are available in smaller sizes as well.

**Features:** rounded or suckering, deciduous shrub or small tree; late-spring to mid-summer flowers; habit; easy to grow **Height:** 3–25' **Spread:** 3–20' **Hardiness:** zones 3–8

# Maple
*Acer*

Maples are appreciated for their dense, shade-producing foliage, neat appearance and near-supernatural, vibrant color in fall. They are hardy, problem-resistant, reliable growers.

## Growing

Generally, maples do well in **full sun** or **light shade**, though this varies from species to species. The soil should be **fertile, moist, high in organic matter** and **well drained**.

## Tips

Use maples as specimen trees, as large elements in shrub or mixed borders or as hedges. Some make useful understory plants bordering wooded areas; others can be grown in containers on patios. Most Japanese gardens have attractive smaller maples. Almost all maples can be used to create bonsai specimens.

## Recommended

*A. rubrum* (red maple) is pyramidal when young, becoming more rounded as it matures. It grows 40–60' tall and has a spread of 35–50'. Cultivars are available including **'Autumn Flame,' 'October Glory'** and **'Red Sunset.'**

*A. saccharum* (sugar maple) is a rounded, pyramidal tree that grows 40–60' tall and 30–50' wide. Newer cultivars include **'Autumn Splendor,' 'Caddo,' 'Commemoration,' 'John Pair'** and **'Legacy.'**

*A. tataricum* (Tatarian maple) is a bushy, deciduous tree with a rounded head. Upright clusters of creamy white flowers are followed by red-winged fruit.

A. rubrum (above), A. ginnala (below)

*A. ginnala* (Amur maple) is a large shrub or small tree. It can be multi-stemmed or trained to a single trunk, and grows 15–20' tall and wide.

*A. truncatum* (Shantung maple) is a medium-sized tree with a rounded shape, maturing to a 25–30' height. The bark is deeply textured and an additional feature of this species.

---

**Features:** small to large, multi-stemmed, deciduous tree or large shrub; foliage; bark; winged fruit; fall color; form; flowers
**Height:** 15–60' **Spread:** 15–50'
**Hardiness:** zones 2–9, varies with the species

# Mock Orange
## *Philadelphus*

*P. coronarius* 'Minnesota Snowflake' (above), *P. coronarius* (below)

Grow mock orange for its heavenly fragrance, which is reminiscent of orange blossoms.

### Growing

Mock oranges grow well in **full sun, partial shade** or **light shade**. The soil should be of **average fertility, humus rich, moist** and **well drained**.

*Mock oranges combine well with forsythias and produce abundant blooms reliably each year.*

### Tips

Include mock oranges in shrub or mixed borders. Use them in groups to create barriers and screens.

### Recommended

*P. coronarius* is an upright, broadly rounded shrub with fragrant, white flowers. It grows tall and wide. Cultivars with variegated or chartreuse foliage are available.

*P. x virginalis* (virginal mock orange) is an upright, medium-sized shrub. It bears single or double, white flowers later than *P. coronarius*. Cultivars are available with large, double flowers.

**Features:** rounded, deciduous shrub with arching branches; early-summer, fragrant, white flowers **Height:** 1½–12' **Spread:** 1½–12' **Hardiness:** zones 3–8

# Mulberry
*Morus*

Some consider this tree to be a weed, but it has many redeeming qualities that make it worth growing, including its tolerance to drought, pollution and poor soils. It's also cold hardy and lovely to look at.

## Growing
Mulberries thrive in **full sun** but can tolerate **partial shade.** The soil should be **well drained** and of **average fertility.** Be careful to prune mulberries in late fall, because any other time would cause them to weep or bleed.

## Tips
Mulberry trees are great specimen trees. Because of their medium size, they're suitable for most gardens and provide deep shade with their dense canopy.

*M. alba* 'Pendula' (left), *M. alba* (above)

## Recommended
*M. alba* (white mulberry) is a spreading tree with heart-shaped leaves that are bright green and glossy. The foliage turns yellow in fall. Fruit-producing selections have white, pink, purple or black fruit in late spring. Fruitless selections are also available, including smaller, ornamental weeping forms.

*Mulberry fruit is acidic to sweet in flavor.*

**Features:** spreading habit, deciduous tree; dense canopy, lush foliage **Height:** 6–40' **Spread:** 8–40' **Hardiness:** zones 4–8

# Ninebark

*Physocarpus*

*P. opulifolius* DIABOLO (above & below)

Ninebark is a tough plant that features attractive foliage and eye-popping, early-summer flowers.

### Growing

Ninebark grows well in **full sun** or **partial shade**. The best leaf coloring develops in a sunny location. The soil should be **fertile, moist** and **well drained**. It adapts well to alkaline soil.

*You may not actually find nine layers, but the peeling, flecked bark of ninebark does add interest to the winter landscape.*

### Tips

Ninebark is an easy-to-grow shrub that adapts to most garden conditions. It can add contrast to a shrub or mixed border, a woodland garden or a naturalistic garden. Ninebark is also useful as an informal hedge.

### Recommended

*P. opulifolius* (common ninebark) is a suckering shrub with long, arching branches and exfoliating bark. It bears light pink flowers in early summer and fruit that ripens to reddish green in fall. Several cultivars are available. **'Dart's Gold'** and **'Nugget'** bear bright yellow foliage. DIABOLO ('Monlo') has attractive purple foliage. SUMMER WINE ('Seward') has dark crimson foliage.

**Features:** upright, sometimes suckering, deciduous shrub; light pink early to mid-summer flowers; fruit; bark; foliage **Height:** 2–10' **Spread:** 2–15' **Hardiness:** zones 2–8

# Oak
*Quercus*

Oaks are the very definition of a majestic tree—their form, foliage, bark and fall color are hard to beat.

## Growing

Oaks grow well in **full sun** or **partial shade**. The soil should be **fertile, moist** and **well drained**. Most oaks prefer **slightly acidic** soil but adapt to alkaline conditions. Oaks can be difficult to establish; transplant them only while they are young.

## Tips

Oaks are large trees that are best as specimens or for groves in parks and large gardens. Do not disturb or compact the rootzone or ground around the base of an oak; this tree is very sensitive to changes in grade and root disturbance.

## Recommended

There are many oaks to choose from. Some of the popular species include *Q. macrocarpa* (bur oak), a large, broad tree with furrowed bark and deeply lobed leaves that turn shades of yellow in fall, growing 60–80' tall and 50–70' wide; *Q. muehlenbergii* (chinkapin oak, yellow chestnut oak) an open, rounded, drought tolerant tree with scaly bark, growing 35–40' tall with an equal to greater spread; *Q. robur* (English oak) is a spreading tree, growing 40–60' tall and 45–65' wide. Numerous cultivars are available including those with columnar habits for smaller gardens. *O. shumardii* (Shumard oak, Texas oak) is a broad columnar tree with spectacular red fall color, growing 60–80' tall and 40–60' wide. It is tolerant of drought conditions.

Q. macrocarpa (above), Q. robur (below)

---

**Features:** large, rounded, spreading, deciduous tree; summer and fall foliage; bark; habit; acorns **Height:** 40–80' **Spread:** 35–70' **Hardiness:** zones 3–9

# Oregon Grape Holly
*Mahonia*

Oregon grape holly can be grown by itself or, better yet, as a transition plant between a woodland garden and a more formal garden. The black berries are edible and can be used to make a wonderful jelly.

### Growing
Oregon grape holly grows in **full sun to light shade**. The soil should be **well drained** and **neutral to slightly acidic**.

### Tips
Use these shrubs in mixed or shrub borders and in woodland gardens. Low-growing specimens can be used as groundcovers.

### Recommended
*M. aquifolium* (Oregon grape holly) is a suckering shrub that produces yellow flowers in spring, followed by clusters of purple or blue berries. The foliage turns a bronze-purple color in late fall and winter. **'Compactum'** is a Pride of Kansas selection that grows 3' high and wide.

*M. repens* (Creeping mahonia) is a low-growing shrub that spreads by suckers. The dull green leaves turn a bronze color in late fall and winter. Small clusters of lightly fragrant, yellow flowers are produced in mid- to late spring, followed by blue-black berries.

*M. aquifolium* (above & below)

**Features:** upright, spreading, evergreen shrub; yellow, late-winter to early-spring flowers; summer fruit; late-fall and winter evergreen foliage **Height:** 1–3' **Spread:** 3–5' **Hardiness:** zones 4–10

# Ornamental Pear

*Pyrus*

Ornamental pear trees flower reliably with a dazzling display of white in spring, followed by shiny dark green foliage and good fall color.

## Growing

Ornamental pear grows best in **full sun.** The soil should be **fertile** and **well drained,** but this tree adapts to most soil conditions and tolerates drought and pollution.

Very little pruning is needed. Remove awkward, crossing and damaged branches in early spring.

## Tips

Ornamental pear makes an excellent specimen tree. The fruit of ornamental pear and its cultivars is not considered edible.

## Recommended

*P. calleryana* is a thorny, irregular, conical tree that is rarely grown in favor of the more popular cultivars. Improvements have been made to the available cultivars, so branches are now less apt to break. 'Aristocrat' is a fast-growing, broadly pyramidal, thornless tree. It has shiny dark green foliage that is tinged purple when young, becoming a brilliant deep red in fall. 'Autumn Blaze' has an irregular, open crown and horizontal branching. It is known for its bright red to purple fall color. 'Capital' is a columnar form that spreads only 5–10'. CHANTICLEER ('Glen's Form,' 'Select,' 'Cleveland Select,' 'Stone Hill') has a narrow, pyramidal form. It blooms profusely in spring, and its leaves turn reddish purple in fall.

*P. calleryana* CHANTICLEER (above)
*P. calleryana* (below)

*Ornamental pear is among the most attractive flowering trees, especially when covered in clouds of white flowers in spring.*

**Also called:** Callery pear **Features:** columnar to broadly pyramidal habit, deciduous; early to mid-spring flowers; fruit; habit; bark; fall foliage **Height:** 30–40' **Spread:** 5–45' **Hardiness:** zones 5–8

# Osage Orange
## Maclura

*M. pomifera* (both photos)

eople often recognize this tree because of its unusual fruit, also known as hedge apple. It stands out in an autumn treeline, displaying dense, green, wrinkled balls of fruit, which is just one of the fine features this tree has to offer, but some people prefer the equally beautiful fruitless selections.

## Growing

Locations in **full sun** are best, while the soil should be **well drained** and of **average fertility.** This durable tree is adaptable to any moisture level.

## Tips

This tough landscape tree has been used as a windbreak or hedge. It's also attractive with a variety of shrubs in a mixed bed or border. Osage orange is an ideal specimen for larger garden settings. Fruitless, thornless varieties are available.

## Recommended

**M. pomifera** is a rounded, deciduous tree that is thorny when young but becomes less so with maturity. It bears bright green foliage that turns yellow in the fall. Tiny yellow-green cup-shaped flowers are borne in longish clusters on female plants, while male trees produce rounded clusters of flowers. Only the female plants produce the wrinkled, rounded, yellow to green fruit. Cultivars are available in variable forms as well as thornless and fruitless selections such as 'Wichita' and 'Whiteshield.'

*The name Osage comes from the Osage tribe, which lived in a limited area centered on the Red River valley in southern Oklahoma and northern Texas. The fruit smells like oranges when it's ripe. Its wood is used to make furniture because it is strong and resistant to rot. Use Osage wood for stepping stones in the garden.*

**Features:** rounded, thorny or thornless, deciduous tree; lush foliage; flower clusters and wrinkled fruit **Height:** 30–40' **Spread:** 20–40' **Hardiness:** zones 4–9

# Pea Shrub
*Caragana*

This plant is hardy to zone 2, holds its own on dry, exposed sites and has the ability to fix nitrogen in the soil. When all other shrubs have succumbed to harsh growing conditions, pea shrub still thrives.

## Growing
Pea shrub prefers **full sun** but will tolerate partial or light shade. Soil of **average to high fertility** is preferred. This plant will adapt to just about any growing conditions and tolerates dry, exposed locations.

## Tips
Pea shrubs are grown as windbreaks and formal or informal hedges. Pea shrubs can also be included in borders, and weeping forms are often used as specimen plants.

## Recommended
*C. arborescens* is a large, twiggy, thorny shrub with upright or arching branches. Yellow, pea-like flowers are borne in late spring, followed by seedpods that ripen to brown in summer and rattle when blown by the wind. Grafted standards that resemble leafy umbrellas are available in various sizes, with either rounded or needle-like leaves. Many cultivars are available including '**Lobergii,**' '**Nana,**' '**Pendula,**' '**Walker**' and '**Sutherland,**' offering varied sizes, forms and habits.

*Pea shrubs are almost impossible to kill. They have superior heat and drought tolerance but fail in locations that are too moist.*

C. arborescens (above & below)

---

**Features:** prickly, grafted, weeping or upright, rounded shrub; late-spring flowers; foliage
**Height:** 3–20' **Spread:** 3–18'
**Hardiness:** zones 2–7

# Pine

*Pinus*

P. flexilis

$\mathcal{P}$ines are such a diverse group of plants that it is hard to know how best to recommend them: are they specimens for hedges or general landscape plants? The answer, of course, is all of the above.

### Growing

Pines grow best in **full sun**. These trees adapt to most **well-drained** soils and are drought tolerant.

Limber pine and Austrian pine, among other species, are prone to *Sphaeropsis* tip blight, but it can be controlled and treated. Consult your local extension department or garden center for treatment options.

### Tips

Pines are more diverse and widely adapted than any other conifers. Pines can be used as specimen trees, as hedges or to create windbreaks. Smaller cultivars can be included in shrub or mixed borders. These trees are not heavy feeders; fertilizing encourages rapid new growth that is weak and susceptible to pest and disease problems.

### Recommended

There are many available pines, both in the form of trees and shrubby dwarf plants. Check with your local garden center or nursery to find out what is available.

The limber pine, *P. flexilis*, is a pyramidal tree when young, maturing to a rounded or flat-topped specimen. It grows 30–40' tall and 15–30' wide, producing very flexible branches. The Austrian pine, *P. nigra*, has often been recommended as the most urban-tolerant pine. It is a pyramidal tree that grows 40–60' tall and 25–40' wide. Lastly, the Southwestern white pine, *P. strobiformis*, has been found to tolerate heat better than the Eastern white pine. It is a pyramidal, symmetrical tree that opens up with age. It gets 40–60' tall and 25–40' wide. It has soft blue-green needles.

**Features:** upright, columnar or spreading, evergreen tree or shrub; foliage; bark; cones; habit **Height:** 30–60' **Spread:** 15–40' **Hardiness:** zones 2–8

# Potentilla

*Potentilla (Pentaphylloides)*

Potentilla is a fuss-free shrub that blooms madly all summer.

## Growing

Potentilla prefers **full sun** but tolerates partial or light shade. The soil should be of **poor to average fertility** and **well drained**. This plant tolerates most conditions, including sandy or clay soil and wet or dry conditions. Established plants are drought tolerant. Too much fertilizer or too rich a soil will encourage weak, floppy, disease-prone growth.

## Tips

Potentilla is useful in a shrub or mixed border. The smaller cultivars can be included in rock gardens and on rock walls. On steep slopes, potentilla can prevent soil erosion and reduce time spent maintaining the lawn. It can even be used to form a low, informal hedge.

If your potentilla's flowers fade in direct sun or hot weather, move the plant to a cooler location with some shade from the hot afternoon sun. Colors should revive in fall as the weather cools. Yellow-flowered plants are least likely to be affected by heat and sun.

## Recommended

Of the many cultivars of *P. fruticosa* (*Pentaphylloides floribunda*), the following are a few of the most popular and interesting. **'Abbotswood'** is one

*P. fruticosa* (above), *P. fruticosa* 'Tangerine' (below)

of the best white-flowered cultivars, **'Gold-finger'** produces lush green foliage, topped with bright yellow flowers, **'Pink Beauty'** bears pink, semi-double flowers, **'Tangerine'** has orange flowers and **'Yellow Gem'** has bright yellow flowers.

---

**Also called:** shrubby cinquefoil, cinquefoil, golden hardhack **Features:** mounding, deciduous shrub; flowers; foliage
**Height:** 3–48" **Spread:** 12–36"
**Hardiness:** zones 2–7

# Privet

*Ligustrum*

*L. amurense* (above & below)

*Many species bloom with fragrant flowers and form persistent berries in fall.*

Privets are among the most used hedge plants of all time, and while they are not ornamentally overwhelming, privets do serve their purpose.

## Growing

Privets grow equally well in **full sun** or **partial shade**. They adapt to any **well-drained** soil and tolerate polluted and urban conditions.

Hedges can be pruned twice each summer. Plants grown in borders or as specimens should be kept neat by removing up to one-third of the mature growth each year.

## Tips

Privets are commonly grown as hedges because they are fast growing, adaptable and inexpensive. Left unpruned, privet can become a large shrub with arching branches. This form looks quite attractive, especially when in bloom.

## Recommended

*L. amurense* (Amur privet) is a large, multi-stemmed shrub that is usually pruned to form a dense hedge. It grows 12–15' tall and spreads 8–15' wide. It bears small white flowers in early to midsummer, followed by small berries that ripen to black. The dark green foliage may turn a dark bronzy purple in fall.

*L. x vicaryi* (golden vicary privet) is a bushy, rounded, semi-evergreen shrub that grows 6–10' tall, with an equal spread. The golden yellow foliage may become more green during hot weather and turns deep purple in fall. Small clusters of white flowers are borne in mid-summer.

**Features:** upright or arching, deciduous or semi-evergreen shrub or tree; adaptability; fast and dense growth **Height:** 6–15' **Spread:** 6–15' **Hardiness:** zones 3–8

# Quince
## *Chaenomeles*

*C. speciosa* 'Texas Scarlet' (above & below)

Beautiful in and out of flower, quince creates an attractive display as a specimen or when trained to grow up or along a brick wall.

## Growing

Quince grows well in **full sun**. It tolerates partial shade but produces fewer flowers. The soil should be of **average fertility, moist, slightly acidic** and **well drained**. These shrubs are tolerant of pollution and urban conditions.

## Tips

Quince can be included in shrub and mixed borders. They are very attractive when grown against a wall, and their spiny habit makes them useful for barriers. Use them along the edge of a woodland or in a naturalistic garden. The dark stems stand out well in winter.

**Features:** spreading, deciduous shrub with spiny branches; red, pink, white, orange spring flowers; fragrant fruit **Height:** 2–5' **Spread:** 2–5' **Hardiness:** zones 5–8

## Recommended

*C. speciosa* is a large, tangled, spreading shrub. It grows 6–10' tall and spreads 6–15' wide. Red, white, pink or coral flowers are borne in late winter, followed by fragrant, greenish yellow fruit. Many cultivars are available, including the popular **'Cameo,'** a low, compact selection with double, apricot-pink blooms, **'Crimson and Gold'** is a low spreading shrub, bearing crimson flowers and growing 3–4' tall and 3' wide, **'Jet Trail'** is also a low grower with pure white blossoms, while **'Texas Scarlet'** produces bright red flowers.

# Redbud
*Cercis*

C. canadensis (above & below)

With its rosy pink cloud of blooms in early spring, redbud is a favorite in almost any home-landscape setting.

## Growing

Redbud will grow well in **full sun, partial shade** or **light shade**. The soil should be a **fertile, deep loam** that is **moist** and **well drained**. This tree is tolerant of wetter areas. It has tender roots and does not like to be transplanted.

Pruning is rarely required. The growth of young plants can be thinned to encourage an open habit at maturity. Remove awkward branches after flowering is complete.

## Tips

Redbud can be used as a specimen tree, in a shrub or mixed border or in a woodland garden.

## Recommended

*C. canadensis* (Eastern redbud) is a spreading, single or multi-stemmed tree that bears pink, red or purple flowers. The young heart-shaped foliage is bronze, fading to green over summer and turning bright yellow in fall. Many beautiful cultivars are available including 'Alba,' also known as whitebud.

*C. reniformis* 'Oklahoma' bears flowers that are dark wine-red in color. The leaves emerge with hints of pale pink before turning green.

*Redbud describes the pointed flower buds, which are slightly deeper in color than the flowers.*

**Features:** rounded or spreading, multi-stemmed, deciduous tree; spring flowers; fall foliage **Height:** 15–30' **Spread:** 15–35' **Hardiness:** zones 4–9

# Rose-of-Sharon

*Hibiscus*

The pros give very clear instructions on the use of this upright shrub: grow it as an informal hedge or in a combined shrub border. Rose-of-Sharon shines in late summer when it shows its interesting colors during the heat-stricken days of July and August.

## Growing

Rose-of-Sharon prefers **full sun**. It tolerates partial shade but becomes leggy and produces fewer flowers. The soil should be **humus rich, moist** and **well drained.** It is tolerant of a variety of conditions, however. Pinch young plants to encourage bushy growth.

Some cultivars are heavy seeders and can produce unwanted offspring. To avoid this problem, shear off and dispose of the seedheads right after blooming finishes.

## Tips

Rose-of-Sharon is best used in shrub or mixed borders. The leaves emerge late in spring and drop early in fall. Plant it with evergreen shrubs to make up for its short period of leafiness.

This plant develops unsightly legs as it matures. Plant low, bushy perennials or shrubs around the base to hide the bare stems.

## Recommended

*H. syriacus* is an erect, multi-stemmed shrub that bears dark pink flowers from mid-summer to fall. It can be trained as a small, single-stemmed tree. Look for the newer cultivars,

*H. syriacus* 'Diana' (above), *H. syriacus* 'Red Heart' (below)

bearing single or double flowers in shades of red, pink, blue, white, lavender, purple and combinations thereof.

**Also called:** Althea **Features:** bushy, upright, deciduous shrub; mid-summer to fall flowers **Height:** 8–12' **Spread:** 6–10' **Hardiness:** zones 5–9

# Russian Olive

*Elaeagnus*

*E. angustifolia* (above & below)

Russian olives are survivors. They can tough it out in dry conditions and even alongside highways bombarded by exhaust and road salt. In a garden setting they can be used in difficult areas with poor-quality soil and great drainage.

## Growing

Russian olives grow best in **full sun**. Ideally, the soil should be a **well-drained**, **sandy loam** of **average to high fertility**. These plants can fix nitrogen from the air and so can adapt to poor soil.

## Tips

Russian olives are used in shrub or mixed borders, as hedges, screens and specimen plants. The fruits are edible but dry and mealy. The branches on some plants can be quite thorny.

## Recommended

*E. angustifolia* is a rounded, spreading tree. The foliage often obscures the fragrant, yellow summer flowers and silvery yellow fruit. The main attractions of this species are its tolerance to adverse conditions and its narrow, silver-gray leaves.

---

**Features:** rounded, spreading, deciduous tree or shrub; fragrant summer flowers; summer foliage; fruit **Height:** 12–20'
**Spread:** 12–20'
**Hardiness:** zones 2–8

# Serviceberry
## *Amelanchier*

Serviceberries generally grow with an open habit that gives the feeling of a naturalized plant. They put on a good show of white flowers in spring, and most produce tasty fruit that attracts a wide range of birds. Fall color is another positive attribute, and its attractive form and branching patterns can be appreciated in winter.

### Growing
Serviceberries grow well in **full sun** or **light shade**. The soil should be **fertile, humus rich, moist** and **well drained**.

### Tips
Serviceberries make beautiful specimen plants or even shade trees in small gardens. The shrubbier forms can be grown along the edges of a woodland or in a border. In the wild, these trees are often found near water sources and are beautiful beside ponds or streams.

### Recommended
The following species have white flowers, purple fruit and good fall color.

*A. alnifolia* (saskatoon serviceberry, alder-leaved serviceberry) is a compact, rounded, suckering shrub that grows 4–6' tall. **'Regent'** is a particularly popular cultivar throughout the state because of its flavorful, juicy fruit.

*A.* **x** *grandiflora* (apple serviceberry) is a small, spreading, often multi-stemmed tree. **'Autumn Brilliance'** is a vigorous selection that grows 20–25' tall and produces stunning fall foliage color.

A. alnifolia 'Regent'

*With a similar but generally sweeter flavor, serviceberry fruit can be used in place of blueberries in any recipe.*

---

**Also called:** saskatoon, juneberry, shadberry **Features:** single- or multi-stemmed, deciduous large shrub or small tree; spring or early-summer flowers; edible fruit; fall color; habit; bark **Height:** 12–25' **Spread:** 12–30' **Hardiness:** zones 3–9

# Smoketree
*Cotinus*

C. coggygria 'Royal Purple' (above), C. coggygria (below)

he 'smoke' is all an illusion. Smoke-tree produces inconspicuous yellow flowers in early summer. When the flower stalks mature, long, feather-like hairs emerge and change to pink or purple, giving the effect of puffs of smoke.

### Growing

Smoketree grows well in **full sun** or **partial shade**. It prefers soil of **average fertility** that is **moist** and **well drained**. Established plants adapt to dry, sandy soils. Smoketree is very tolerant of alkaline, gravel-like soil.

### Tips

Smoketree can be used in a shrub or mixed border, as a single specimen or in groups. It is a good choice for a rocky hillside planting.

### Recommended

*C. coggygria* is a bushy, rounded shrub that develops large, puffy plumes of flowers that start out green and gradually turn a pinky gray. The green foliage turns red, orange and yellow in fall. Many cultivars are available. **'Flame'** has purple-pink flowers and bluish green foliage that turns bright orange-red in fall. **'Nordine'** ('Nordine Red') is the hardiest of the purple-leaved cultivars. It has pink flowers, showy red fruit and plum-purple foliage. **'Royal Purple'** (purple smokebush) has purplish red flowers and dark purple foliage.

*C. obovatus* (American smoketree) is a broadly conical shrub or small tree with grayish brown bark and oval leaves that are pink-bronze when young, maturing to shades of brilliant orange, red and purple in the fall. Pinkish, plume-like fruiting panicles are borne in summer. This species grows 25' tall and 20' wide.

**Also called:** smokebush **Features:** bushy, rounded, spreading, deciduous tree or shrub; early-summer flowers; summer and fall foliage; easy to grow **Height:** 8–30' **Spread:** 8–25' **Hardiness:** zones 4–8

# Spirea
*Spiraea*

S. *japonica* 'Little Princess' (above), S. x *vanhouttei* (below)

Spireas are old-fashioned shrubs that became cutting-edge choices when dwarf, colorful types were introduced. They are becoming even more popular now that groundcover species have joined the mix.

## Growing

Spireas prefer **full sun**. To help prevent foliage burn, spireas should be protected from very hot sun. The soil should be **fertile, acidic, moist** and **well drained**.

## Tips

Spireas are popular because they adapt to a variety of situations and once established require only minimal care. They are used in shrub or mixed borders, in rock gardens and as informal screens and hedges.

## Recommended

Many species and cultivars are available including the following three popular selections. **S.** *japonica* (Japanese spirea) forms a clump of erect stems and bears pink or white flowers. It is parent to a plethora of colorful cultivars. **S. x van-houttei** (bridal wreath spirea, Vanhoutte spirea) is a dense, bushy shrub with arching branches that bears clusters of white flowers and **S.** *thunbergii* (Thunberg spirea) is a dense, arching shrub, growing 3–5' tall and wide. Small clusters of white flowers appear along the stems in spring before the leaves emerge. Check with your local nursery or garden center to see what is available.

**Features:** round, bushy, deciduous shrub; summer flowers; habit **Height:** 2–10' **Spread:** 2–12' **Hardiness:** zones 3–9

# Spruce
*Picea*

*P. glauca* var. *densata* (left), *P. glauca* (above)

### Growing
Spruce trees grow best in **full sun to partial shade**. The soil should be **deep, well drained** and **moist**. Spruces are best grown from small, young stock as they dislike being transplanted when larger or more mature.

### Tips
Spruce trees are used as specimens. These trees look most attractive when allowed to keep their lower branches. This tree can also be used as a hedge or windbreak when planted in rows.

### Recommended
*P. glauca* var. *densata* (Black Hills spruce) produces dark green needles that may have a hint of blue. It has a dense-branching, symmetrical habit and pyramidal form. This slow-growing species grows 30–40' tall and 15–20' wide.

Renowned for their excellent, tall, conical growth habits, trees of the genus *Picea* add an element of formality to the garden. Grow them where they have enough room to spread, then let them branch all the way to the ground.

*Stradivarius used spruce to make his renowned violins, and the resonant, lightweight but tough wood is still preferred for violins, guitars, harps and the sounding boards of pianos.*

**Features:** pyramidal, evergreen tree; foliage; cones; habit **Height:** 30–40' **Spread:** 15–20' **Hardiness:** zones 2–6

# St. Johnswort

*Hypericum*

*H. frondosum* 'Sunburst' (left), *H. frondosum* (above)

Masses of bright yellow flowers with numerous, showy, hair-like stamens add sunshine to the summer garden.

## Growing

St. Johnsworts grow best in **full sun** but tolerate partial shade. **Well-drained** soil of **average fertility** is preferred, but these plants adapt to most soil conditions except wet soils. They also tolerate drought and heavy, rocky or very alkaline soils.

## Tips

St. Johnsworts make good additions to mixed or shrub borders, where the late-summer flowers can brighten up a planting that is looking tired or faded in the heat of summer. These durable shrubs are also useful for areas where the soil is poor and watering is difficult.

## Recommended

**H. frondosum** (golden St. Johnswort) forms a rounded, upright mound. This deciduous species grows 2–4' tall, with an equal spread. Bright yellow flowers are borne in mid- and late summer. The long, dense stamens give each flower a fuzzy appearance. **'Sunburst'** is a frequently recommended cultivar.

---

**Also called:** St. John's Wort
**Features:** summer to fall flowers; attractive foliage; tidy, rounded, deciduous or evergreen shrub **Flower color:** yellow **Height:** 2–4'
**Spread:** 2–5' **Hardiness:** zones 5–9

*Many medicinal and magical properties have been attributed to species of St. Johnswort. It is currently used to treat mild forms of depression.*

# Sumac

*Rhus*

R. typhina (above), R. aromatica (below)

Sumacs are long lived, often spreading and always easy to grow. The season-long foliage displays outstanding form and color, with many varieties putting forth a stellar fall show of brilliant yellows, oranges and reds. They also make good wildlife habitat.

## Growing

Sumacs develop the best fall color in **full sun** but tolerate partial shade. The soil should be of **average fertility, moist** and **well drained**. Once established, sumacs are very drought tolerant.

These plants can become invasive. Remove suckers that come up where you don't want them.

## Tips

Sumacs can be used in a shrub or mixed border, in a woodland garden or on a sloping bank. Both male and female plants are needed for fruit to form.

## Recommended

*R. aromatica* (fragrant sumac) is a low mounding, suckering sumac that grows 2–6' tall and 5–10' wide. It bears aromatic foliage and clusters of inconspicuous yellow flowers in spring, followed in late summer by fuzzy fruit that ripens to red.

*R. glabra* (smooth sumac) grows 8–12' tall, with an equal or greater spread and forms a bushy, suckering colony. Green summer flower spikes are followed, on female plants, by fuzzy red fruit. The foliage turns brilliant shades of orange, red and purple in the fall.

*R. typhina* (*R. hirta;* staghorn sumac) is a suckering, colony-forming shrub whose branches are covered with velvety fuzz. The species grows 15–25' tall and spreads 25' or more. Fuzzy, yellow, early-summer blooms are followed by hairy red fruit. The leaves turn stunning shades of yellow, orange and red in fall. **'Bailtiger'** (TIGER EYES) has finely cut, burn-resistant, golden yellow foliage.

---

**Features:** bushy, suckering, colony-forming, deciduous shrub; summer and fall foliage; chartreuse summer flowers; fuzzy, red, fall fruit **Height:** 2–25' **Spread:** 5–25' or more; often exceeds height **Hardiness:** zones 2–9

# Sweetspire

*Itea*

Sweetspire is valued for the fragrance from its showy, elongated bottle-brush flower clusters. Vibrant fall color is another reason to use sweetspire.

## Growing

Sweetspire grows well in all light conditions from **full sun** (best fall color) **to full shade** (less arching, more upright habit). The soil should be **fertile** and **moist,** although sweetspire is fairly adaptable. Chlorosis (leaf yellowing) may occur in highly alkaline soils or during drought.

## Tips

Sweetspire is an excellent shrub for low-lying and moist areas. It grows well near streams and water features. It is also a fine choice for plantings in areas where the scent of the fragrant flowers can be enjoyed. Sweetspire can be used individually or in small groups in the home garden, and it looks awesome mass planted in large areas.

## Recommended

*I. virginica* is an upright to arching, suckering shrub that usually grows wider than tall. Spikes of fragrant, white flowers appear in late spring. The leaves turn shades of purple and red in fall. **'Henry's Garnet,'** a Pride of Kansas selection, has larger flowers than the species and bright reddish purple fall color.

*I. virginica* 'Henry's Garnet' (above), *I. virginica* (below)

*Sweetspire has been refined from its wild, straggly habit, and recent cultivars offer neat, compact additions to the shrub border.*

**Features:** upright to arching, deciduous shrub; fragrant, white flowers; fall color
**Height:** 2–6'  **Spread:** 3–6' or more
**Hardiness:** zones: 5–9

# Viburnum

*Viburnum*

*V. carlesii* (left), *V. opulus* (above)

f you have room for just one shrub in the landscape, make it a viburnum. These attractive shrubs come in many shapes and sizes. Almost all are hardy and easy to care for, with multi-season interest.

## Growing

Viburnums grow well in **full sun, partial shade** or **light shade**. The soil should be of **average fertility, moist** and **well drained**. Viburnums tolerate alkaline and acidic soils.

Deadheading keeps these plants looking neat but prevents fruits from forming. Fruiting is better when more than one plant of a species is grown.

## Tips

Viburnums can be used in borders and woodland gardens.

*Viburnums feature a wide assortment of attractive foliage choices and ornate, often fragrant flowers.*

## Recommended

Many species, hybrids and cultivars are available. A few popular ones include *V. carlesii* (Korean spice viburnum), a dense, bushy, rounded, deciduous shrub with white or pink spice-scented flowers, *V.* 'Emerald Triumph' grows 10' tall and wide, bearing glossy but textured foliage, creamy clusters of flowers followed by colorful fruit, *V. opulus* is a rounded, spreading, deciduous shrub with lacy-looking flower clusters. 'Roseum' (snowball viburnum) produces round white flower clusters that resemble snowballs, *V. prunifolium* (Blackhaw viburnum) is a round-headed tree or large shrub with glossy, bright green foliage that changes to bronze, followed by red in fall. It produces creamy white flowers, followed by edible, pinkish-colored fruit that matures to bluish black. This species grows 12–15' tall and 8–12' wide.

**Features:** bushy or spreading, evergreen, semi-evergreen or deciduous shrub; flowers (some fragrant); summer and fall foliage; fruit; habit **Height:** 6–15' **Spread:** 6–12' **Hardiness:** zones 2–9

# Weigela
*Weigela*

Weigela earns its way into Kansas gardens because of its striking, long-lasting bloom. The bright, trumpet-shaped flowers attract hummingbirds.

## Growing

Weigela prefers **full sun** but tolerates partial shade. For the best leaf color, grow purple-leaved plants in full sun and yellow-leaved plants in partial shade. The soil should be **fertile** and **well drained**. Weigela adapts to most well-drained soils.

## Tips

Weigelas can be used in shrub or mixed borders, in open woodland gardens and as informal barrier plantings.

## Recommended

*W. florida* is a spreading shrub with arching branches that bear clusters of dark pink flowers. Many hybrids and cultivars are available, including dwarf varieties, red-, pink- or white-flowered varieties and varieties with purple, bronze or yellow foliage. **'Minuet'** is a compact, spreading shrub, 2–3' tall and 3–4' wide. The dark pink flowers have yellow throats. The purplish green foliage matures to dark green over summer. **'Pink Poppet'** is a dwarf selection with a compact, rounded habit, bright green foliage and an abundance of pale pink flowers. **'Ruby Queen'** is a semi-dwarf cultivar with reddish burgundy leaves, a rounded growth habit and bright pink flowers. WINE & ROSES ('Alexandra') has dark purple foliage and vivid pink flowers.

*W. florida* WINE & ROSES (above), *W. florida* (below)

*Weigela is one of the longest-blooming shrubs, with the main flush of blooms lasting as long as six weeks. It often re-blooms if sheared lightly after the first flowers fade.*

**Features:** upright or low, spreading, deciduous shrub; late-spring to early-summer flowers; foliage; habit **Height:** 1–6' **Spread:** 2–6' **Hardiness:** zones 3–8

# Yew

*Taxus*

*T. x media* 'Densiformis' (above), *T. x media* (below)

Yews are the great forgivers of the evergreen garden. They can be shaped to whatever form you desire—from formal hedges to whimsical topiary figures. Their uses are nearly limitless, and their tolerance is almost inexhaustible.

## Growing

Yews grow well in **full sun to full shade**. The soil should be **fertile, moist** and **well drained**. Yews dislike very wet soil and soil that is contaminated with road salt. Do not plant them near downspouts or

other places where water collects. These evergreens tolerate windy, dry and polluted conditions.

## Tips

Yews can be used in borders or as specimens, hedges, topiaries and groundcover. Male and female flowers are borne on separate plants. Both must be present for the attractive red arils (seed cups) to form.

## Recommended

*T.* **x** *media* (English Japanese yew), a cross between *T. baccata* (English yew) and *T. cuspidata* (Japanese yew), has the vigor of the English yew and the cold hardiness of the Japanese yew. It forms a rounded, upright tree or shrub, though the size and form varies among the many cultivars. Three of the more popular selections in Kansas are 'Brownii,' 'Densiformis' and 'Hicksii.'

---

**Features:** evergreen; conical or columnar tree, or bushy or spreading shrub; foliage; habit; red seed cups **Height:** 2–50' **Spread:** 1–30' **Hardiness:** zones 4–7

# Bonica

## Modern Shrub Rose

Bonica was the first modern shrub rose to be named an All-America Selection. The blooms have a light and sweet fragrance. Bright orange hips follow the double pink flowers.

### Growing

Bonica prefers **full sun** and **fertile, moist, well-drained** soil with at least **5% organic matter** mixed in. It can tolerate light breezes, but keep it out of strong winds. Roses are heavy feeders and drinkers and do not like to share their root space with other plants. This disease-resistant, hardy rose tolerates afternoon shade and poor soils.

### Tips

Bonica suits just about any location. Rose growers recommend it for mixed beds, containers, hedges, cut-flower gardens or as a groundcover, standard or specimen.

### Recommended

*Rosa* **'Bonica'** is a tidy, spreading rose of modest size that blooms profusely throughout most of the growing season. It bears an abundance of semi-glossy, rich green foliage that is beautiful enough to stand on its own.

*This beautiful rose has maintained worldwide popularity since its introduction in 1982.*

**Also called:** Bonica '82, Meidomonac, Demon, Bonica Meidiland **Features:** repeat blooming, medium pink summer to fall flowers; easy maintenance; colorful hips **Height:** 3–5' **Spread:** 3–4' **Hardiness:** zones 4–9

# Crimson Glory
## Hybrid Tea Rose

*F*or many years this hybrid tea rose has been one of the most reliable red selections available on the market because of its blooming habit, disease resistance and fragrant blossoms.

### Growing
A location in **full sun** is best. The soil should be **well drained, moist** and **nutrient rich** for Crimson Glory to thrive. This hybrid tea rose will benefit from a judicious pruning annually to encourage a more upright habit and bushy form.

### Tips
This medium-sized rose is ideal for mixed borders and beds. It would also make a lovely informal, flowering hedge. The flowers are great for cutting.

### Recommended
*Rosa* 'Crimson Glory' bears large, double flowers, reaching 4–4¹/₂" wide. Each flower is made up of 30 petals or more, is very fragrant and has a classic form. Crimson Glory is known to have good all-season bloom.

*This moderately thorny rose was the Royal National Rose Society Gold Medal winner in 1936, and the James Alexander Gamble Rose Fragrance Medal winner in 1961.*

**Features:** deep, velvety red, double flowers; lush, dark, disease resistant foliage; habit
**Height:** 3½–4'  **Spread:** 3–4'
**Hardiness:** zones 5–9

# Don Juan
## Climbing Rose

This large-flowered, climbing rose is definitely the 'Don Juan' of red bloomers—it draws you in and teases your senses.

### Growing
Don Juan prefers to grow in locations with **full sun** but will tolerate partial sun. The soil should be of **moderate to high fertility, well drained** and **moist.**

### Tips
This rose is ideal for growing against walls with a support, including a trellis, netting, railing, or pillars along or atop staircases.

### Recommended
*Rosa* **'Don Juan'** is a large, deciduous shrub, reaching 8–10' heights. It produces 4½–5" wide, double blossoms that are very sweetly scented, in a high-centered, hybrid tea form. Don Juan is a reliable repeat bloomer and each flower is made up of at least 35 petals. This vigorous, upright selection is clothed in lush, dark green foliage that is resistant to disease.

*This rose was created by Malandrone in Italy and released in the U.S. in 1958. It is the result of crossing a 'New Dawn' seedling with 'New Yorker.'*

---

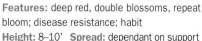

**Features:** deep red, double blossoms, repeat bloom; disease resistance; habit
**Height:** 8–10'  **Spread:** dependant on support
**Hardiness:** zones 5–9

# Fragrant Cloud
## Hybrid Tea Rose

*A*lthough its full, bright, orangy red flowers are beautiful in their own right, Fragrant Cloud is best known for its outstanding, unique fragrance.

### Growing
Fragrant Cloud prefers **full sun** and **fertile, moist, well-drained** soil with at least **5% organic matter** mixed in. Light breezes are tolerable, but keep roses out of strong winds. Roses are heavy feeders and drinkers, and do not like to share their root space with other plants.

Fragrant Cloud is mildly prone to mildew in the fall and blackspot in damp weather.

### Tips
Fragrant Cloud is ideal for borders and beds. It requires very little maintenance other than seasonal deadheading and a little spring pruning. Cool weather produces the best flower color.

### Recommended
*Rosa* 'Fragrant Cloud' is bushy and upright, with well-branched canes and glossy, dark green foliage. It bears typical, high-centered, double, hybrid tea flowers made up of more than 30 petals each.

*Fragrant Cloud has been showered with numerous honors and awards, mostly in recognition of its outstanding scent.*

**Also called:** Nuage Parfume
**Features:** repeat blooming, orangy red, summer to fall flowers; fragrance; size
**Height:** 4–5'  **Spread:** 32–36"
**Hardiness:** zones 5–9

# Knockout

Modern Shrub/Landscape Rose

This rose is simply one of the best new shrub roses to hit the market in years.

### Growing
Knockout grows best in **full sun**. The soil should be **fertile, humus rich, moist** and **well drained**. This rose blooms most prolifically in warm weather but has deeper red flowers in cooler weather. Deadhead lightly to keep the plant tidy and to encourage prolific blooming.

### Tips
This vigorous rose makes a good addition to a mixed bed or border, and it is attractive when planted in groups of three or more. It can be mass planted to create a large display, or grown singly as an equally beautiful specimen.

### Recommended
*Rosa* 'Knockout' has a lovely, rounded form with glossy, green leaves that turn to shades of burgundy in fall. The bright cherry red flowers are borne in clusters of 3–15 almost all summer and into fall. Orange-red hips last well into winter. **'Double Knockout,' 'Pink Knockout'** and a light pink selection called **'Blushing Knockout'** are available.

*If you've been afraid that roses need too much care, you'll appreciate the hardiness and disease resistance of this low-maintenance beauty.*

---

**Features:** rounded habit; light, tea-rose scent; mid-summer to fall flowers in shades of pink or red; disease resistant **Height:** 3–4' **Spread:** 3–4' **Hardiness:** zones 4–10

# Nearly Wild
## Floribunda Rose

Nearly Wild is one of the hardiest floribunda roses and one of the first to bloom in the spring.

### Growing
Nearly Wild prefers **full sun** but can tolerate partial shade. The soil should be of **average to poor fertility**, **moist** and **well drained**.

### Tips
Though it looks wild, its growth habit is quite tame. The plant is nicely rounded and dense, making it ideal as a short hedge.

### Recommended
*Rosa* **'Nearly Wild'** bears small, long, pointed buds that open into single, medium pink blossoms with a central white eye. The moderately sweet, apple-scented blossoms are made up of five petals each, resulting in a simple yet classic form. The flowers are borne in clusters on long, straight stems atop a bushy form. Nearly Wild blooms prolifically, and the flowers almost totally obscure the foliage underneath.

*This rose was hybridized by H.C. Brownell in 1941. If introduced today, this tough little rose would probably be sold as a shrub rose.*

---

**Features:** 2–2½" wide, medium pink flowers with a white eye, repeat blooming habit and hardiness **Height:** 24–36" **Spread:** 24–36" **Hardiness:** zones 4–10

# New Dawn

Climbing Rose

$\mathcal{I}$ ntroduced in 1930, New Dawn is still a favorite climbing rose of gardeners and rosarians alike.

## Growing

New Dawn grows best in **full sun**. The soil should be **average to fertile, humus rich, moist** and **well drained**. This rose is disease resistant.

## Tips

Train New Dawn to climb pergolas, walls, pillars, arbors, trellises and fences. With some judicious pruning, this rose can be trained to form a bushy shrub or hedge. Deadheading will encourage further blooming or a repeat bloom. Plant it where the blooms will welcome visitors to your home.

## Recommended

*Rosa* 'New Dawn' is a vigorous climber with upright, arching canes and glossy, green foliage. Singly or in small clusters, it bears pale pink flowers.

---

**Features:** glossy, green foliage; climbing habit; long blooming period; pale, pearl-pink flowers with a sweet, apple-like fragrance
**Height:** 10–15' **Spread:** 10–15'
**Hardiness:** zones 4–9

# Rainbow's End

Miniature Rose

Rainbow's End is considered one of the most beautiful miniature roses ever developed and is ranked the most popular miniature available today.

## Growing

Rainbow's End prefers **full to partial sun.** The soil should be **well drained,** of **average fertility** and **moist.**

Generally resistant to disease, this rose is a little prone to blackspot.

## Tips

With its bushy and upright form, Rainbow's End is best in the garden rather than in a decorative container in the house. However, it does suit decorative containers on the patio and deck. It is suitable for cut-flower gardens, beds or borders.

## Recommended

*Rosa* **'Rainbow's End'** bears pointed buds that open into double, classic hybrid tea-type blooms in deep yellow shades touched with dark pinky red. The pinky red color will intensify in full sun, creating a distinctive edge. Age can also influence the intensity, and the entire petal may turn almost completely red. The flowers are lightly scented. Sturdy maroon stems support small, dark, glossy leaves with burgundy, serrated edges. This rose has a rounded and compact, well-branched and upright form.

**Features:** deep yellow, double flowers with dark pinky red edges; miniature habit
**Height:** 12–16"  **Spread:** 10–14"
**Hardiness:** zones 4–11

# Sally Holmes

Modern Shrub Rose

It's easy to be impressed by the magnificent flowers, but the most beautiful feature of this rose is its balance—one feature isn't more prominent than another; all the features work together, resulting in a beautiful package.

## Growing

This rose thrives in **full sun** but tolerates partial shade. The soil should be of **average to high fertility, well drained** and consistently **moist.**

Deadhead early in the season to prolong the blooming cycle. The petals will fall cleanly from each stem, resulting in a well-formed hip.

## Tips

This highly disease-resistant rose is easily trained as a climber along a fence or wall in warmer locations. It is effective as a specimen and blends well with a variety of flowering plants in mixed beds and borders.

## Recommended

*Rosa* 'Sally Holmes' bears large trusses of single creamy white flowers lightly touched with peach. The flowers fade over time until they are almost pure white when fully open. The clusters are enormous, each stem carrying 50 or more blooms on graceful arching canes. Each flower is made up of five petals that open flat to expose prominent stamens. The flowers are complemented by large, semi-glossy, pointed leaves.

---

**Features:** creamy white, single flowers with peach undertones, lightly scented; habit; size **Height:** 3–5' **Spread:** 3–5' **Hardiness:** zones 5–9

# Sevilliana

## Modern Shrub Rose

Sevilliana was developed by the illustrious rose breeder, Dr. Griffith Buck. Buck roses are always representative of hardiness, beauty, reliability, fragrance and simplicity, and Sevilliana is no exception.

### Growing

Locations in **full** or **partial sun** are best for Sevilliana. **Well-drained, moist** soil of **average to high fertility** is ideal.

### Tips

This modern shrub rose has something to offer almost all year-round. It repeat blooms throughout the spring and summer followed by bright, colorful hips in the fall and into winter. Mixed beds and borders are sure to be complemented with this beauty. Even the fall color is spectacular.

### Recommended

*Rosa* '**Sevilliana**' is a medium-sized shrub, growing up to 4' tall and wide. It produces lush green foliage that emerges green with copper hues until the leaves harden off or mature. Large clusters of pointed buds emerge in late spring that open into light pink, semi-double, cup-shaped blooms, with yellow at the base of each flower. Each flower is fragrant and made up of 15–20 petals.

*'Sevilliana' commemorates the music and the dancing of Seville, Spain.*

**Features:** colorful, fragrant flowers, repeat bloom; copper-tinted foliage when young; winter hardy; reliability **Height:** 4' **Spread:** 4' **Hardiness:** zones 4–10

# Scentimental

Floribunda Rose

The red and white striped flowers of Scentimental are almost as alluring as their spicy fragrance.

## Growing

Scentimental grows best in **full sun** in a warm, sheltered location. Soil should be **fertile, humus rich, moist** and **well drained.** Amending the soil with additional organic matter will improve its nutrient content, texture, water retention and drainage.

## Tips

Scentimental has a neat rounded form that makes it an excellent specimen plant as well as a lovely addition to a mixed border.

## Recommended

*Rosa* 'Scentimental' is a shrubby, rounded plant with large dark green leaves. It produces fully double flowers for most of the summer.

**Features:** shrubby habit; red and white striped summer to fall flowers **Height:** 3–4' **Spread:** 3–4' **Hardiness:** zones 4–9

# Sunsprite

## Floribunda Rose

Sunsprite is one of the best yellow floribunda roses, not only for color and habit but for fragrance as well. It was an award winner in Baden-Baden in part for its outstanding scent.

### Growing

Sunsprite prefers to grow in locations with **full sun.** Partial sun is tolerated. The soil should be **well drained, humus rich** and **moist.**

Only minimal maintenance is required, including an annual pruning and adequate mulching. Deadhead to keep the plant neat and tidy.

### Tips

It is easily grown as a standard or as low, colorful hedging and is one of the best bedding roses available. This rose is disease resistant and vigorous. A new climbing form now available is best used on arbors and trellises.

### Recommended

*Rosa* **'Sunsprite'** produces bright lemon yellow, double flowers. The flowers maintain long-lasting color without fading. Each flower is made up of 28 or more symmetrically arranged petals. The highly fragrant flowers are quite large in size, reaching 3–3$^{1}/_{2}$" widths. The glossy foliage becomes stocky and compact over time.

*The blooms are known to shatter quite quickly after opening, so flowers are better left on the plant.*

**Other names:** Friesia **Features:** licorice-scented, brightly colored blossoms; habit; disease resistance; repeat bloom
**Height:** 30–36"  **Spread:** 24"
**Hardiness:** zones 5–11

# Bittersweet Vine

*Celastrus*

Bittersweet vine is a rough-and-tumble, low-maintenance vine with a wilder appearance than other plants in the Kansas landscape.

## Growing

Bittersweet vine grows well in **full sun** but tolerates partial shade. It adapts to almost any well-drained soil. **Poor** soil is preferred, because rich soil can create a monster. Bittersweet vine needs little to no pruning.

Male and female flowers usually bloom on separate plants. For assured fruit production, in addition to regular watering, both males and females need to be planted close together.

## Tips

Bittersweet vine is a great choice for the edge of a woodland garden or in naturalized areas. It quickly covers old trees, fences, arbors, trellises, posts and walls. It can mask piles of rubble and old tree stumps. It effectively controls erosion on hard-to-maintain slopes.

## Recommended

*C. scandens* is a deciduous twining vine or sprawling groundcover with glossy, dark green foliage that turns bright yellow in fall. Small, undistinguished, yellow-green to whitish flowers bloom in late spring. The orange seeds are enclosed by bright red arils (seed cups). '**Diana**' and '**Hercules**' are an example of a compatible female and male pair.

*The berries dry beautifully for use in floral arrangements.*

**Also called:** American bittersweet, staff vine **Features:** fast growth; decorative fruit; fall color **Height:** 20–30' **Spread:** 3–6' **Hardiness:** zones 2–8

*C. scandens* (above & below)

# Clematis
*Clematis*

C. 'Etoile Violette' (above), C. x *jackmanii* (below)

*Plant two clematis varieties together that bloom at the same time to provide a mix of color and texture, or allow one to run through your climbing roses.*

Clematis is one of the most rewarding plants that can be grown in a home garden. There are so many species, hybrids and cultivars of clematis that it is possible to have one in bloom at any point in the season.

## Growing

Clematis plants thrive in **full sun** and tolerate partial shade. Afternoon shade is best. The soil should be **fertile, humus rich, moist** and **well drained**. They enjoy warm, sunny weather but prefer to have cool roots. A thick layer of mulch or a planting of low, shade-providing perennials around the base will protect the tender roots. Clematis are quite cold hardy but fare best when protected from winter wind. The rootball should be planted about 2" beneath the soil surface.

## Tips

Clematis vines can climb up structures such as trellises, railings, fences and arbors. They can also be allowed to grow over shrubs and up trees and can be used as groundcover.

## Recommended

There are many species, hybrids and cultivars of clematis. The flower forms, blooming times and sizes of the plants vary. Check with your local garden center to see what is available.

**Also called:** virgin's bower **Features:** twining habit; blue, purple, pink, yellow, red, white early- to late-summer flowers; decorative seedheads **Height:** 8–30' **Spread:** 2–4' **Hardiness:** zones 4–8

# Climbing Hydrangea

*Hydrangea*

*H. anomala* subsp. *petiolaris* (above & below)

A mature climbing hydrangea can cover an entire wall, and with its dark, glossy leaves and delicate, lacy flowers, it is possibly one of the most stunning climbing plants available.

## Growing

Climbing hydrangeas grow well in **full to partial shade.** Leaves and flowers can scorch in full sun. The soil should be of **average to high fertility, humus rich, moist** and **well drained.** These plants perform best in cool, moist conditions.

## Tips

Climbing hydrangea climbs up trees, walls, fences, pergolas and arbors. It clings to walls by means of aerial roots, so it needs no support, just a somewhat textured surface. It also grows over rocks and can be used as a groundcover—or train it to form a small tree or shrub. It can be slow to get established.

## Recommended

*H.* **anomala** subsp. *petiolaris* (*H. petiolaris*) is a clinging vine with dark, glossy green leaves that sometimes turn an attractive yellow in fall. In early summer, the vine is covered with white, lacy-looking flowers—the entire plant appears to be veiled in a lacy mist. These plants produce the most flowers when exposed to some direct sunlight each day.

---

**Features:** white flowers; clinging habit; exfoliating bark **Height:** 50–80'
**Spread:** 50–80' **Hardiness:** zones 4–9

# Grape
*Vitis*

*V. coignetiae*

The grape vine's bold foliage and colorful fruit provide a look of maturity to a garden and a feel of permanence and weight that many new gardens need.

### Growing
Grapes require **full sun** in a warm, south-facing location. The soil should be **deep, moist** and **acidic**. Choose a location that warms quickly in spring. Grape vines need to be pruned and trained annually for the best fruit production and to keep the plants tidy. Winter protection is often required. Grapes are sensitive to an assortment of herbicides.

*Kansas currently has more than 90 vineyards and more than 170 acres devoted to grape growing.*

### Tips
Grape vines can be trained to grow on almost any sturdy structure. They may need to be tied in place until the basic structure is established.

### Recommended
*V. coignetiae* (crimson glory vine) a vigorous, ornamental, woody, deciduous climber. It produces large, heart-shaped leaves, coarsely textured and toothed and dark green in color throughout the growing season, and turns a brilliant crimson red in fall. This species will grow up to 50' tall and wide with support. Small bluish black grapes are produced in fall but are considered to be unpalatable. A variety of cultivars and hybrids are grown for their edible fruit, including **'Concord,' 'Fredonia,' 'Frontenac,' 'Niagara'** and **'Sunbelt.'**

**Features:** edible fruit; summer foliage; long-lived, woody, climbing, deciduous vine **Height:** 30–50' **Spread:** 30–50' **Hardiness:** zones 3–9

# Honeysuckle
## *Lonicera*

The colorful, tropical look and fragrance of honeysuckle blooms are reason enough to grow this popular, long-lived vine, but the blooms are also attractive to butterflies and hummingbirds.

### Growing

Honeysuckles grow well in **full sun** but tolerate partial shade. The soil should be **average to fertile, humus rich, moist** and **well drained**.

### Tips

Honeysuckle vines are twining, deciduous climbers that can be trained to grow up a trellis, fence, arbor or other structure. They can spread as widely as they climb to fill the space provided.

### Recommended

*L.* x *brownii* (scarlet trumpet honeysuckle, Brown's honeysuckle) bears showy but unscented red or orange flowers (zones 5–8). **'Dropmore Scarlet'** bears bright red tubular flowers.

*L.* x *heckrottii* (goldflame honeysuckle) is a deciduous to semi-evergreen vine with attractive blue-green foliage. It bears fragrant pink and yellow flowers.

*L. japonica* (Japanese honeysuckle) is a vigorous, woody, evergreen or semi-evergreen twining climber. It produces paired, dark green leaves and exotic, fiery-colored flowers, followed by blue-black berries. Many cultivars are available including **'Halliana'** ('Hall's honeysuckle), producing fragrant white flowers that age to a dark yellow color.

L. *sempervirens* (above), L. x *heckrottii* (below)

*L. sempervirens* (trumpet honeysuckle, coral honeysuckle) bears orange, yellow or red flowers. Cultivars such as **'Alabama Crimson'** and **'John Clayton'** set red fruit in the fall.

**Features:** orange, red, yellow, pink, spring, summer or fall flowers; twining habit; fruit **Height:** 10–20' **Spread:** 10–20' **Hardiness:** zones 3–8

# Hyacinth Bean
*Lablab (Dolichos)*

*L. purpureus* (above & below)

Think of hyacinth beans as sweet peas on steroids. The vines grow profusely and provide great visual interest, including flowers and iridescent purple seed pods.

### Growing
Hyacinth bean prefers **full sun**. The soil should be **average to fertile, moist** and **well drained**. Feed it regularly to encourage plentiful flowering.

*The raw beans contain a cyanide-releasing chemical, so never eat the beans unless they are thoroughly cooked, using two to four changes of water.*

If starting from seed, soak seed overnight to speed germination. Direct sow seeds around the last-frost date, or start indoors in peat pots in early spring.

### Tips
Hyacinth bean needs a trellis, net, pole or other structure to twine up. Plant it against a fence or near a balcony. If you grow it as a groundcover, make sure it doesn't engulf smaller plants.

### Recommended
*L. purpureus (Dolichos lablab)* is a vigorously twining vine. It can grow up to 30' tall, but it only reaches about 10–15' tall when grown as an annual. It bears many purple or white flowers over summer, followed by deep purple pods.

**Also called:** Egyptian bean, lablab bean, lablab, Indian bean **Features:** large, bold leaves; habit; sweet-pea-like, purple or white flowers; purple seedpods **Height:** 10–15' **Spread:** variable **Hardiness:** treat as an annual

# Silver-Lace Vine
*Polygonum*

This charming vine is perfect for softening the edges of wooden structures such as decks, lattices and fences.

## Growing
Silver-lace vine grows well in **full sun, partial shade** or **light shade**. The soil should be of **average to poor fertility, moist** and **well drained**. This plant requires a sturdy support to twine around.

## Tips
This fast-growing vine is useful for creating screens, especially on chain-link fences. It can also be trained up an arbor, pergola or trellis. Its vigor makes it valuable in tough-to-garden areas, but it can become weedy in more fertile conditions.

## Recommended
*P. aubertii (Fallopia aubertii)* is a fast-growing, twining, woody climber. Clusters of small, white flowers are produced in late summer and stand out attractively against its heart-shaped leaves. This vigorous grower can overwhelm other vegetation, so make sure you place it where it can grow up a sturdy structure and not over neighboring plants.

*P. aubertii* (above & below)

*Silver-lace vine roots where the branches touch the ground, and new plants can sprout from the small pieces of root left in the ground.*

**Also called:** mile-a-minute plant, fleece vine **Features:** twining deciduous vine; attractive, white summer flowers; foliage **Height:** 25–40' or more **Spread:** 25–40' or more **Hardiness:** zones 4–8

# Trumpet Vine
*Campsis*

*C. radicans* (above), *C. radicans* cultivar (below)

Trumpet vine is a chugging locomotive of a plant that will cover just about anything and everything in its path.

## Growing

These heat-tolerant vines grow well in full sun, partial shade or light shade but flower best in **full sun**. They will grow in any soil, but growth is most rampant in **fertile** soil.

## Tips

Trumpet vine clings to any surface—a wall, a tree, a fence or a telephone pole. One plant can provide a privacy screen very quickly, or it can be grown up an exterior wall or over the porch of a house. Trumpet vine can be used on arbors and trellises but needs frequent pruning to stay attractive and within bounds. Once you have one of these vines, you will probably never get rid of it.

## Recommended

***C. radicans*** is a fast-growing, deciduous vine that bears dark orange, trumpet-shaped flowers for a long period in summer. **'Flava'** bears yellow flowers.

*Hummingbirds are attracted to the long, tube-like flowers of trumpet vine.*

---

**Also called:** trumpet creeper
**Features:** clinging habit; orange, red, yellow summer flowers **Height:** 10–30'
**Spread:** 10–30' **Hardiness:** zones 5–9

# Virginia Creeper • Boston Ivy

*Parthenocissus*

Virginia creeper and Boston ivy are handsome vines that establish quickly and provide an air of age and permanence, even on new structures.

## Growing

These vines grow well in any light, from **full sun to full shade**. The soil should be **fertile** and **well drained**. The plants will adapt to clay or sandy soils.

## Tips

Virginia creepers do not require support because they have clinging rootlets that adhere to just about any surface, even smooth wood, vinyl or metal. Give the plants a lot of space and let them cover a wall, fence or arbor.

## Recommended

These two species are very similar, except for the shape of the leaves.

*P. quinquefolia* (Virginia creeper, woodbine) has dark green foliage that turns flame red in fall. Each leaf is divided into five leaflets.

*P. tricuspidata* (Boston ivy, Japanese creeper) has dark green, three-lobed leaves that turn red in fall. This species is not quite as hardy as Virginia creeper, zones 4–8.

*Virginia creeper and Boston ivy can cover the sides of buildings and help keep them cool in the summer heat. Cut the plants back as needed to keep windows and doors accessible.*

*P. tricuspidata* 'Fenway Park' (above)
*P. quinquefolia* (below)

**Features:** summer and fall foliage; clinging habit **Height:** 30–70' **Spread:** 30–70' **Hardiness:** zones 3–9

# Wisteria
*Wisteria*

*W. floribunda* 'Alba' (above) *W. floribunda* (below)

Loose clusters of purple flowers hang like lace from the branches of wisteria. With careful pruning, a gardener can create beautiful tree forms and attractive arbor specimens.

## Growing
Wisterias grow well in **full sun** or **partial shade**, though blooming may be reduced in partial shade. The soil should be of **average fertility, moist** and **well drained**. Too fertile a soil will produce lots of vegetative growth but very few flowers. Avoid planting wisteria near a lawn where fertilizer may leach over to your vine.

## Tips
These vines require something sturdy to twine around, such as an arbor or pergola. Select a permanent site, because wisterias don't like to be moved. They may send up suckers and can root wherever the branches touch the ground. All parts of wisteria are poisonous.

## Recommended
*W. floribunda* (Japanese wisteria) is a vigorous, twining climber with large leaves made up of many smaller leaflets. It produces pea-like, bluish purple or white, fragrant flowers in pendent clusters. The species grows up to 25' tall and wide. Many cultivars are available with dark purple, pink and white flowers.

**Features:** blue, purple, pink, white late-spring flowers; attractive foliage; twining habit
**Height:** 25'  **Spread:** 25'
**Hardiness:** zones 5–9

# Allium

*Allium*

*A. sphaerocephalum*

 llium has an other-worldly
appearance that is sure to attract
attention in the garden: striking, ball-
like to loose, nodding clusters of flowers
on tall stems.

## Growing

Alliums grow best in **full sun**. The soil
should be **average to fertile, moist** and
**well drained**. Plant bulbs in fall, 2–4" deep,
depending on the size of the bulb.

## Tips

Alliums are best planted in groups in a
bed or border where they can be left to
naturalize. Most will self-seed when left
to their own devices. The foliage, which
tends to fade just as the plants come into
flower, can be hidden with groundcover
or a low, bushy companion plant.

**Also called:** flowering onion **Features:** pink,
purple, white, yellow, blue, maroon summer
flowers; cylindrical or strap-shaped leaves
**Height:** 1–6' **Spread:** 2–12"
**Hardiness:** zones 3–9

## Recommended

Several allium species, hybrids and cultivars have gained popularity for their
decorative, pink, purple, white, yellow,
blue or maroon flowers. These include
*A. caeruleum* (blue globe onion), with
globe-like clusters of blue flowers;
*A. cristophii* (stars of Persia) with strap-
shaped foliage and a large, rounded
cluster of 100 or more star-shaped,
pinkish purple flowers with a metallic
sheen; *A. giganteum* (giant onion), a big
plant that grows up to 6' tall, with large,
globe-shaped clusters of pinky purple
flowers; *A. moly* (golden garlic, lily leek),
which produces strap-like leaves with
golden yellow orb-like flowers made up
of 30 or more star-shaped flowers; and
*A. sphaerocephalum* (drumstick allium,
round-headed garlic), which produces
mid-green foliage and clusters of 40 or
more tightly packed, bell-shaped flowers
in green to pink, to reddish brown.

# Caladium

*Caladium*

C. x *hortulanum* cultivar (above)
C. x *hortulanum* 'Sweetheart' (below)

The mid-ribs and veining of the caladium only strengthen the design, helping draw the eye to the smashing leaf colors. If you are searching for bold texture in the garden, caladiums are a must.

## Growing

Caladiums prefer to grow in **partial to full shade** in **moist, well-drained, humus-rich, slightly acidic** soil.

Caladiums are tuberous plants that can be grown from seed or from the tubers. Start growing tubers inside in a soil-less planting mix with a temperature at a minimum of 70° F. Once they have leafed out they can handle cooler soil temperatures of a minimum of 55° F. When planting out, add a little bone-meal or fishmeal to the planting hole. Make sure the knobby side of the tuber is facing up and is level with the soil surface or just under.

## Tips

Caladiums will give a tropical feel to your garden. They do very well around water features and in woodland gardens. They are equally effective in the herbaceous border en masse or as specimens and are wonderful plants for containers. The tubers are tender and must be dug up, when grown in the ground, and brought inside for winter and kept at 50–60° F. When grown in containers there is no need to dig the tubers in fall. Simply bring the whole container inside for the winter.

All parts of caladium may irritate the skin, and ingesting this plant will cause stomach upset.

## Recommended

***C.* x *hortulanum*** (*C. bicolor*) is native to the edge of woodlands in tropical South America. The often tufted, arrow-shaped foliage is dark green and variously marked and patterned with red, white, pink, green, rose, salmon, silver or bronze. Each leaf is 6–12" long.

**Also called:** elephant's ears, heart-of-Jesus, mother-in-law plant, angel wings
**Features:** ornate, patterned and colorful foliage; habit **Height:** 18–24" **Spread:** 18–24"
**Hardiness:** treat as an annual.

# Calla Lily
## *Zantedeschia*

This beautiful, exotic-looking plant was only available as a cut flower in the past. The introduction of new cultivars, however, has made it more readily available and worth planting.

## Growing

Calla lilies grow best in **partial shade.** The soil should be **fertile, humus rich** and **moist.** Callas grown in containers can be brought indoors for winter. Reduce watering in winter, keeping the soil just moist.

## Tips

Calla lilies are ideal additions to mixed beds and borders, and work well as container specimens. Calla lilies are also a great addition to the water garden, because they will thrive in wet locations and can even be partially submerged into shallow water.

Rather than moving large, cumbersome plants, it is sometimes easier to remove small divisions in fall and transfer them indoors over the winter.

## Recommended

**Z. aethiopica** (white arum lily, white calla) forms a clump of arrow-shaped, glossy green leaves. It bears white flowers from late spring to mid-summer. Several cultivars are available.

**Z. elliottiana** (yellow calla, golden calla) forms a basal clump of white-spotted, dark green, heart-shaped leaves. It grows 24–36" tall and spreads 8–12". This species bears yellow flowers in summer and is a parent plant of many popular hybrids.

*Z. aethiopica* 'Little Gem' (above)
*Z. elliottiana* hybrid (below)

*Although they grow quite large, calla lilies can be grown as houseplants year-round but benefit from being outdoors in summer.*

Features: white, yellow flowers; foliage
Height: 16–36" Spread: 8–24"
Hardiness: treat as an annual

# Canna
*Canna*

Cannas are stunning, dramatic plants that give an exotic flair to any garden.

## Growing

Cannas grow best in **full sun** in a **sheltered** location. The soil should be **fertile, moist** and **well drained**. Plant out in spring once soil has warmed. Plants can be started early indoors in containers to get a head start on the growing season. Deadhead to prolong blooming.

## Tips

Cannas can be grown in a bed or border. They make dramatic specimen plants and can even be included in large planters.

## Recommended

A wide range of cannas are available, including cultivars and hybrids with green, bronzy, purple or yellow and green striped foliage. Flowers may be white, red, orange, pink, yellow or bicolored. Dwarf cultivars that grow 18–28" tall are also available.

C. 'Red King Humbert' (above & below)

*The rhizomes can be lifted after the foliage dies back in fall. Clean off any clinging dirt, cut off foliage and store them in a cool, frost-free location in peat moss. Check on them regularly through winter and if they begin to sprout, pot them and place them near a bright window until they can be moved outdoors.*

**Features:** decorative foliage; white, red, orange, pink, yellow, bicolored summer flowers **Height:** 18"–6' **Spread:** 12–36" **Hardiness:** zones 7–9; treat as an annual

# Crocus

*Crocus*

C. x *vernus* cultivars (above & below)

Crocuses are harbingers of spring. They often appear, as if by magic, in full bloom from beneath the melting snow.

## Growing

Crocuses grow well in **full sun** or **light, dappled shade**. The soil should be of **poor to average fertility, gritty** and **well drained**. The corms are planted about 3" deep in fall.

## Tips

Crocuses are almost always planted in groups. Plant drifts of crocuses in lawns to provide interest and color while the grass still lies dormant. They can be left to naturalize in beds and borders. Groups of plants will fill in and spread out to provide a bright welcome in spring.

## Recommended

Many crocus species, hybrids and cultivars are available. The spring-flowering crocus most people are familiar with is *C.* x *vernus,* commonly called Dutch crocus. *C. sativus* (saffron crocus) is a fall-blooming species with deep purple flowers detailed with dark purple veins, zones 3–6. *C. speciosus* is another fall-blooming species with with long, tubed flowers in shades of purple-blue with deep blue veins. Many cultivars are available, with flowers in shades of purple, yellow or white, sometimes bicolored or with darker veins.

**Features:** purple, yellow, white, sometimes bicolored, early-spring flowers **Height:** 2–6"
**Spread:** 2–4" **Hardiness:** zones 3–8

# Daffodil

*Narcissus*

N. hybrids (above & below)

Many gardeners automatically think of large, yellow, trumpet-shaped flowers when they think of daffodils, but there is plenty of variation in color, form and size among the daffodils.

## Growing

Daffodils grow best in **full sun** or **light, dappled shade**. The soil should be **average to fertile, moist** and **well drained**. Bulbs should be planted in fall, about 6" deep, depending on the size of the bulb. The bigger the bulb, the deeper it should be planted. A rule of thumb is to measure the bulb from top to bottom and multiply that number by three to know how deep to plant.

## Tips

Daffodils are often planted where they can be left to naturalize —or spread—in the light shade beneath a tree or in a woodland garden. In mixed beds and borders, the daffodils' faded leaves will be hidden by the summer foliage of other plants.

## Recommended

Many species, hybrids and cultivars of daffodils are available. Flowers come in shades of white, yellow, peach, orange, pink, red and green and may also be bicolored. Flowers range from $1^1/_2$–6" across, solitary or borne in clusters. About 13 flower-form categories have been defined.

**Features:** white, yellow, peach, orange, pink, red, green, or bicolored spring flowers
**Height:** 4–24"  **Spread:** 4–12"
**Hardiness:** zones 3–9

# Gladiolus

### *Gladiolus*

*P*erhaps best known as a cut flower, gladiolus adds an air of extravagance to the garden.

## Growing

Gladiolus grows best in **full sun** but tolerates partial shade. The soil should be **fertile, humus rich, moist** and **well drained**. Flower spikes may need staking and a sheltered location out of the wind to prevent them from blowing over.

Plant corms in spring, 4–6" deep, once soil has warmed. Corms can also be started early indoors. Plant a few corms each week for about a month to prolong the blooming period.

## Tips

Planted in groups in beds and borders, gladiolus make a bold statement. Corms can be dug and stored in peat moss in a cool, frost-free location.

## Recommended

*Gladiolus* **hybrids** have flowers that come in almost every imaginable shade, except blue. Plants are commonly grouped in three classifications: **Grandiflorus** is the best known, each corm producing a single spike of large, often ruffled flowers; **Nanus**, the exception, survives in zone 3 with protection and produces several spikes of up to 7 flowers; **Primulinus** produces a single spike of up to 23 flowers that grow more spaced out than those of the grandiflorus.

*G. x hortulanus* Grandiflorus (above)
*G.* 'Homecoming' (below)

*Over 10,000 hybrid cultivars of Gladiolus have been developed.*

Features: brightly colored, mid- to late-summer flowers in almost every color except blue
Height: 18"–6' Spread: 6–12"
Hardiness: zone 8; grown as an annual

# Grape Hyacinth
*Muscari*

M. *botryoides* (above), M. *armeniacum* (below)

Daffodils should never be alone to signal the emergence of spring. Grape hyacinth bulbs are the perfect accompaniment with other spring flowers. They contrast beautifully with just about any color combination.

## Growing

Grape hyacinth prefers **full sun to partial shade**. The soil should be **well drained** and **organically rich**.

## Tips

Grape hyacinth is great for naturalizing. Plant individual bulbs random distances from one another in lightly wooded areas and mixed borders, 5–6" deep. Grape hyacinths are also quite beautiful planted alongside perennials that are tall enough to envelope the tired-looking foliage once they reach their full size. Plant grape hyacinth around other bulbs

and hostas as markers to ensure that these other bulbs aren't forgotten about and dug up. The leaves of grape hyacinth emerge in fall.

## Recommended

*M. armeniacum* (Armenian grape hyacinth) produces grass-like foliage and clusters of purple-blue, grape-like flowers atop slender green stems. The flowers emit a strong, musky scent. **'Blue Spike'** produces double blue flowers, and **'Heavenly Blue'** has sky blue flowers. **'Valerie Finnis'** is the best of all, bearing silvery blue flowers.

*M. botryoides* (common grape hyacinth) has a form that is slightly more compact. It is less aggressive than other species and will naturalize in a more respectable manner. It bears flowers in blue, pink or white.

*M. latifolium* is a bulbous perennial with semi-erect, mid-green foliage and dense, upright clusters of purple-black flowers and crowns of flowers paler in color.

**Features:** grape-like clusters of fragrant, blue flowers; habit **Height:** 6–10" **Spread:** 6–8" **Hardiness:** zones 2–8

# Lily

*Lilium*

Decorative clusters of large, richly colored blooms grace these tall plants. Flowers are produced at differing times of the season, depending on the hybrid, so it is possible to have lilies blooming all season if a variety of cultivars is chosen.

## Growing

Lilies grow best in **full sun** but like to have their **roots shaded**. The soil should be rich in **organic matter, fertile, moist** and **well drained**.

## Tips

Lilies are often grouped in beds and borders and can be naturalized in woodland gardens and near water features. These plants are narrow but tall; plant at least three plants together to create some volume.

## Recommended

The many species, hybrids and cultivars available are grouped by type. Visit your local garden center to see what is available. The following are two popular groups of lilies. **Asiatic Hybrids** bear clusters of flowers in early or mid-summer and are available in a wide range of colors. **Oriental Hybrids** bear clusters of large, fragrant flowers in mid- and late summer. Colors are usually white, pink or red.

*L.* Asiatic Hybrids (above), *L.* 'Stargazer' (below)

*Lily bulbs should be planted in fall before the first frost but can also be planted in spring if bulbs are available, including Easter lilies.*

Features: early-, mid- or late-season flowers in shades of orange, yellow, peach, pink, purple, red, white Height: 2–5' Spread: 12" Hardiness: zones 4–7

# Tulip
*Tulipa*

*T. hybrids (above & below)*

Tulips, with their beautiful, often garishly colored flowers, are a welcome sight as we enjoy the warm days of spring.

### Growing
Tulips grow best in **full sun**. In light or partial shade the flowers tend to bend toward the light. The soil should be **fertile** and **well drained**. Plant bulbs in fall, 6–8" deep, depending on the size of the bulb. Bulbs that have been cold treated can be planted in spring. Although tulips can repeat bloom, many hybrids perform best if planted new each year.

### Tips
Tulips provide the best display when mass planted or planted in groups in flowerbeds and borders. They can also be grown in containers and can be forced to bloom early in pots indoors. Some of the species and older cultivars can be naturalized in meadow and wildflower gardens.

### Recommended
There are about 100 species of tulips. The thousands of hybrids and cultivars are generally divided into 15 groups, according to bloom time and flower appearance. They come in dozens of shades with many bicolored or multi-colored varieties. Blue is the only shade not available. Check with your local garden center in early fall for the best selection.

*During the tulipomania of the 1630s, the bulbs were worth many times their weight in gold, and many tulip speculators lost their fortune when the mania ended.*

Features: spring flowers  Height: 6–30"
Spread: 2–8"  Hardiness: zones 3–8; sometimes treated as annuals

# Basil

*Ocimum*

The sweet, fragrant leaves of fresh basil add a delicious, licorice-like flavor to pesto, salads and tomato-based dishes.

## Growing

Basil grows best in a **warm, sheltered** location in **full sun**. The soil should be **fertile, moist** and **well drained**. Pinch tips regularly to encourage bushy growth. Plant out or direct sow seed after frost danger has passed in spring.

For best flavor, keep tops of plants pinched back to keep the basil from flowering.

## Tips

Although basil grows best in a warm spot outdoors in the garden, it can be grown successfully indoors in a pot by a bright window to provide you with fresh leaves all year.

## Recommended

*O. basilicum* is one of the most popular of the culinary herbs. There are dozens of varieties, including ones with large or tiny, green or purple and smooth or ruffled leaves.

*O. basilicum* 'Genovese' and 'Cinnamon' (above)
*O. basilicum* 'Genovese' (below)

*Certain cultivars are used for different culinary purposes, including 'Genovese' for pesto, 'Cinnamon' for desserts and 'Sweet Dani' for a nice complement to most lemony flavored dishes.*

*Basil is a good companion plant for tomatoes—both like warm, moist growing conditions and when you pick tomatoes for a salad you'll also remember to include a few sprigs or leaves of basil.*

---

**Features:** fragrant, decorative leaves **Height:** 12–24" **Spread:** 12–18" **Hardiness:** tender annual

# Chives
*Allium*

A. schoenoprasum (above & below)

*Chives are said to increase appetite and encourage good digestion.*

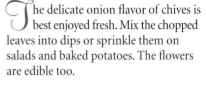

The delicate onion flavor of chives is best enjoyed fresh. Mix the chopped leaves into dips or sprinkle them on salads and baked potatoes. The flowers are edible too.

### Growing
Chives grow best in **full sun**. The soil should be **fertile, moist** and **well drained,** but chives adapt to most soil conditions. These plants are easy to start from seed, but they do like the soil temperature to stay above 66° F before they will germinate, so seeds started directly in the garden are unlikely to sprout before early summer.

### Tips
Chives are decorative enough to be included in a mixed or herbaceous border and can be left to naturalize. In an herb garden, chives should be given plenty of space to allow self-seeding.

### Recommended
*A. schoenoprasum* forms a clump of bright green, cylindrical leaves. Clusters of pinky purple flowers are produced in early and mid-summer. Varieties with white or pink flowers are available.

*A. tuberosum* (Chinese chives, garlic chives) are similar in appearance to the former species but slightly different in flavor, resembling garlic.

*Chives will spread with reckless abandon as the clumps grow larger and the plants self-seed. Chives are also great to divide and share with friends.*

---

**Features:** foliage; form; pinkish purple flowers
**Height:** 8–24"  **Spread:** 12" or more
**Hardiness:** zones 3–8

# Dill
*Anethum*

Dill leaves and seeds are probably best known for their use as pickling herbs, although they have a wide variety of other culinary uses.

## Growing

Dill grows best in **full sun** in a **sheltered** location out of strong winds. The soil should be of **poor to average fertility, moist** and **well drained**. Sow seeds every couple of weeks in spring and early summer to ensure a regular supply of leaves. Plants should not be grown near fennel because the plants will cross-pollinate and the seeds will lose their distinct flavors.

## Tips

With its feathery leaves, dill is an attractive addition to a mixed bed or border. It can be included in a vegetable garden but does well in any sunny location. It also attracts butterflies and beneficial insects.

## Recommended

*A. graveolens* forms a clump of feathery foliage. Clusters of yellow flowers are borne at the tops of sturdy stems.

*A. graveolens* (above & below)

*A popular Scandinavian dish called gravalax is made by marinating a fillet of salmon in brine flavored with the leaves and seeds of dill.*

**Features:** feathery, edible foliage; yellow summer flowers; edible seeds **Height:** 2–5' **Spread:** 12" or more **Hardiness:** annual

# Fennel
*Foeniculum*

F. vulgare (above), F. vulgare 'Purpureum' (below)

*Fennel has been used for its medicinal and culinary properties since before ancient Greek times.*

All parts of fennel are edible and have a distinctive, licorice-like fragrance and flavor. The seeds are commonly used to make a tea that is good for settling the stomach after a large meal.

## Growing

Fennel grows best in **full sun**. The soil should be **average to fertile, moist** and **well drained**. Avoid planting fennel near dill and coriander, because cross-pollination reduces seed production and makes the seed flavor of each herb less distinct. Fennel easily self-sows.

## Tips

Fennel is an attractive addition to a mixed bed or border, and it can be included in a vegetable garden. It also attracts pollinators and beneficial insects to the garden. To collect the seeds, remove the seedheads before the seeds start to fall off. It's important to dry them before storing to keep them from getting musty.

## Recommended

*F. vulgare* is a short-lived perennial that forms clumps of loose, feathery foliage. Clusters of small, yellow flowers are borne in late summer. The seeds ripen in fall. **Var. *azoricum*** (Florence fennel) is an annual or biennial that forms a large, edible bulb at the stem base. This bulb is popular raw in salads, cooked in soups or stews and roasted like other root vegetables. **'Purpureum'** or **'Rubrum'** (bronze fennel) have bronzy purple foliage and are similar in appearance to the species but provide food for the caterpillars of swallowtail butterflies.

**Features:** attractive, fragrant foliage; yellow late-summer flowers; decorative seeds **Height:** 2–6' **Spread:** 12–24" **Hardiness:** zones 5–9

# Mint

*Mentha*

The cool, refreshing flavor of mint lends itself to tea and other hot or cold beverages. Mint sauce, made from freshly chopped leaves, is often served with lamb.

## Growing
Mint grows well in **full sun** or **partial shade**. The soil should be **average to fertile, humus rich** and **moist**. These plants spread vigorously by rhizomes and should be planted in pots if you don't want them to spread throughout your yard.

## Tips
Mint is a good groundcover for damp or neglected spots and along ditches that may only be periodically wet. It also can be used in beds and borders but may overwhelm less vigorous plants.

The flowers attract bees, butterflies and other pollinators to the garden. Mint is also said to repel ants.

For best flavor, keep tops of plants pinched back to keep them from flowering.

## Recommended
There are many species, hybrids and cultivars of mint. Spearmint (**M. spicata**), peppermint (**M. x piperita**) and orange mint (**M. x piperita** var. **citrata**) are three of the most commonly grown culinary varieties. More decorative varieties have variegated or curly leaves, and other varieties have unusual, fruit-scented leaves.

*M. piperita* 'Chocolate' (above)
*M. piperita* var. *citrata* (below)

*A few sprigs of fresh mint added to a pitcher of iced tea give it an extra zip.*

**Features:** fragrant foliage; purple, pink, white summer flowers **Height:** 6–36" **Spread:** 36" or more **Hardiness:** zones 4–8

# Oregano
*Origanum*

O*regano is one of the best-known and most frequently used herbs. It is popular in tomato-based sauces, stuffings, soups and stews, and no pizza is complete until it has been sprinkled with fresh or dried oregano leaves.

### Growing
Oregano grows best in **full sun**. The soil should be of **poor to average fertility** and **well drained**. The flowers attract pollinators to the garden.

### Tips
These bushy herbs make a lovely addition to any border and also ideal container plants.

### Recommended
*O. vulgare hirtum* (oregano, Greek oregano) is the most flavorful culinary variety of oregano. This low, bushy plant has hairy, gray-green leaves and bears white flowers. Many other interesting varieties are available, including those with golden, variegated or curly leaves. **Var. 'Kaliteri'** (Kaliteri oregano) grows 2' tall and wide and is known for its high oil content, pungent flavor and aroma.

O. vulgare 'Aureum' (above & below)

*In Greek,* oros *means 'mountain,' and* ganos *means 'joy' or 'beauty,' so oregano translates as 'joy' or 'beauty of the mountain'.*

**Features:** fragrant foliage; white or pink summer flowers; bushy habit **Height:** 12–32" **Spread:** 8–18" **Hardiness:** zones 5–8

# Rosemary
*Rosmarinus*

The needle-like leaves of rosemary are used to flavor a wide variety of foods, including chicken, pork, lamb, rice, tomato and egg dishes.

## Growing
Rosemary prefers **full sun** but tolerates partial shade. The soil should be of **poor to average fertility** and **well drained**.

## Tips
In a mild winter, rosemary will survive in the ground and often even in a pot left outside. Low-growing, spreading selections can be included in a rock garden, grown along the top of a retaining wall or grown in hanging baskets.

## Recommended
*R. officinalis* is a dense, bushy, evergreen shrub with narrow, dark green leaves. The habit varies somewhat between cultivars from strongly upright to prostrate and spreading. Flowers are usually in shades of blue, but pink-flowered cultivars are available. Plants rarely reach their mature size when grown in containers.

*R. officinalis (above & below)*

*To overwinter a container-grown plant indoors, keep it in very light or partial shade in summer, then put it in a sunny window indoors for winter and keep it well watered but not soaking wet.*

**Features:** fragrant, evergreen foliage; bright blue, sometimes pink, summer flowers
**Height:** 8"–4' **Spread:** 1–4' **Hardiness:** zone 6; usually grown as an annual

# Sage
## *Salvia*

S. *officinalis* 'Icterina' (above)
S. *officinalis* 'Purpurea' (below)

Sage is perhaps best known as a flavoring for stuffing, but it has a great range of uses in soups, stews, sausages and dumplings.

## Growing

Sage prefers **full sun** but tolerates light shade. The soil should be of **average fertility** and **well drained**. These plants benefit from a light mulch of compost each year. They are drought tolerant once established.

## Tips

Sage is an attractive plant for borders. It can be used to add volume to the middle of a border, or as an attractive edging or feature plant near the front. Sage can also be grown in mixed planters.

## Recommended

S. *officinalis* is a woody, mounding plant with soft gray-green leaves. Spikes of light purple flowers appear in early and mid-summer. Many cultivars with attractive foliage are available, including the silver-leaved 'Berggarten,' the yellow-margined 'Icterina,' the purple-leaved 'Purpurea' and the purple-green and cream variegated 'Tricolor,' which has a pink flush to the new growth.

*Sage has been used as a medicinal and culinary herb since at least as early as ancient Greek times.*

**Features:** fragrant decorative foliage; blue or purple summer flowers **Height:** 12–24" **Spread:** 18–36" **Hardiness:** zones 4–7

# Tarragon
*Artemisia*

The distinctive licorice flavor of tarragon lends itself to a wide variety of meat and vegetable dishes and is the key flavoring in bearnaise sauce.

## Growing
Tarragon grows best in **full sun**. The soil should be **average to fertile, moist** and **well drained**. Divide the plants every few years to keep them growing vigorously and to encourage the best leaf flavor.

## Tips
Tarragon is not exceptionally decorative. It can be included in an herb garden or mixed border where its tall stems will be supported by the surrounding plants.

## Recommended
*A. dracunculus* var. *sativa* is a bushy plant with tall stems and narrow leaves. Airy clusters of insignificant flowers are produced in late summer.

*Before purchasing a plant, chew a leaf to see if it has the distinctive flavor you seek. French tarragon is the preferred culinary selection, whereas Russian tarragon (A. d. var.* dracunculoides*) is a more vigorous plant but has little of the desired flavor.*

*A. dracunculus* var. *sativa* (above & below)

---

**Features:** narrow, fragrant leaves; airy flowers
**Height:** 18–36" **Spread:** 12–18"
**Hardiness:** zones 3–8

# Thyme
*Thymus*

T. vulgaris (above), T. x citriodorus (below)

Thyme is at the forefront of the latest gardening trends—this petite perennial is not just a herb, it is now considered a highly valuable ornamental plant.

### Growing
Thyme prefers **full sun**. The soil should be of **poor to average fertility**. **Good drainage** is essential. It is beneficial to work organic matter into the soil to improve structure and drainage.

### Tips
Thyme is useful for sunny, dry locations at the front of borders, between or beside paving stones, on rock gardens and rock walls, and in containers.

Once the plants have finished flowering, shear them back by about half to encourage new growth and to prevent the plants from becoming too woody.

### Recommended
*T.* **x** *citriodorus* (lemon-scented thyme) forms a mound of lemon-scented, dark green foliage. The flowers are pale pink. Cultivars with silver- or gold-margined leaves are available.

*T. vulgaris* (common thyme) forms a bushy mound of dark green leaves. The flowers may be purple, pink or white. Cultivars with variegated leaves are available.

*These plants attract bees when in bloom. Thyme honey is pleasantly herbal and goes very well with biscuits.*

---

**Features:** creeping or bushy habit; fragrant, decorative foliage; purple, pink, white flowers
**Height:** 4–18" **Spread:** 10–16"
**Hardiness:** zones 4–8

# Ajuga
*Ajuga*

*A. reptans* 'Caitlin's Giant' (above & below)

Why have grass when you can cover the ground with these lovely ramblers? Often described as rampant runners, ajugas grow best where they can roam freely.

## Growing

Ajugas develop the best leaf color in **partial** or **light shade** but tolerate full shade; excessive sun may scorch the leaves. Any **well-drained** soil is suitable. Divide these vigorous plants any time during the growing season.

When growing hybrids with fancy leaf coloration, remove any new growth or seedlings that revert to green.

## Tips

Ajugas make excellent groundcovers for difficult sites, such as exposed slopes and dense shade. They are also attractive in shrub borders, where their dense growth prevents the spread of all but the most tenacious weeds.

## Recommended

*A. pyramidalis* 'Metallica Crispa' (upright bugleweed) is a very slow-growing plant with bronzy, crinkly foliage and violet blue flowers.

*A. reptans* is a low, quick-spreading groundcover. The many cultivars are grown for their colorful, often variegated foliage.

**Also called:** bugleweed **Features:** purple, pink, bronze, green, white variegated foliage; late-spring to early-summer flowers in purple, blue, pink, white **Height:** 3–12" **Spread:** 6–36" **Hardiness:** zones 3–8

# Cinnamon Fern
*Osmunda*

Ferns have a certain prehistoric mystique and can add a graceful elegance and textural accent to the garden.

## Growing

Cinnamon ferns prefer **light shade** but tolerate full sun if the soil is consistently moist. The soil should be **fertile, humus rich, acidic** and **moist,** but wet soil is tolerated. Cinnamon ferns spread as offsets form at the plant bases.

## Tips

Cinnamon ferns forms an attractive mass when planted in large colonies. They can be included in beds and borders. Cinnamon ferns also make a welcome addition to a woodland garden.

## Recommended

*O. cinnamomea* has light green sterile fronds that fan out in a circular fashion from a central point. The leafless, bright green fertile fronds appear in spring standing straight up in the center of the plant; they mature to cinnamon brown.

*O. cinnamomea* (above & below)

*The cinnamon fern's 'flowers' are actually its spore-producing sporangia.*

**Also called:** flowering fern
**Features:** perennial deciduous fern; decorative fertile fronds; habit **Height:** 30"–5'
**Spread:** 2–3' **Hardiness:** zones 2–9

# Dead Nettle

*Lamium*

*L. maculatum* 'Lime Light' (above), *L. maculatum* 'Beacon Silver' (below)

These attractive plants, with their striped, dotted or banded foliage, hug the ground and thrive in the barest conditions.

## Growing

Dead nettles prefer **partial to light shade;** although they tolerate full sun, they may become leggy. The soil should be of **average fertility, humus rich, moist** and **well drained**. The more fertile the soil, the more vigorously the plants grow. When grown in the shade, these plants tolerate drought, but they can develop bare patches if the soil is allowed to dry out for extended periods. Divide and replant in autumn if any bare spots become unsightly.

Dead nettles remain more compact if sheared back after flowering.

**Features:** decorative, often variegated foliage; spring or summer flowers in white, pink, yellow, or mauve **Height:** 4–24" **Spread:** indefinite **Hardiness:** zones 3–8

## Tips

These plants make useful groundcovers for woodland or dry shade gardens. They also work well under shrubs in a border, where the dead nettles help keep weeds down.

## Recommended

*L. galeobdolon* (*Lamiastrum galeobdolon*; yellow archangel) can be quite invasive, although the several available cultivars are less so. The yellow flowers appear from spring to early summer.

*L. maculatum* (spotted dead nettle) is the most commonly grown dead nettle. This low-growing, spreading species has green leaves with white or silvery markings and bears white, pink or mauve flowers. Many cultivars are available.

# English Ivy
*Hedera*

*H. helix* (above & below)

One of the loveliest things about English ivy is the variation in green tones it adds to the garden.

## Growing

English ivy prefers **light shade** or **partial shade** but will adapt to any light conditions, from full shade to full sun. The foliage can become damaged or dried out in winter if the plant is grown in a sunny, exposed site. The soil should be of **average to rich fertility, moist** and **well drained**. The richer the soil, the better this vine will grow.

## Tips

English ivy is grown as a trailing groundcover or as a climbing vine. It clings tenaciously to house walls, tree trunks, stumps and many other rough-textured surfaces. Ivy rootlets can damage walls and fences, so be careful to select a good location for this plant.

## Recommended

*H. helix* is a vigorous plant with dark, glossy, triangular, evergreen leaves that may be tinged with bronze or purple in winter, adding another season of interest to your garden. Many cultivars have been developed, some for increased cold hardiness and others for their interesting, often variegated foliage. Check with your local garden center to see what is available.

*English ivy is also a popular houseplant and is frequently used in topiaries.*

**Also called:** common ivy **Features:** foliage; climbing or trailing habit **Height:** indefinite **Spread:** indefinite **Hardiness:** zones 5–8

# Feather Reed Grass

*Calamagrostis*

This graceful metamorphic grass changes its habit and flower color with the seasons. The slightest breeze sets this grass in motion.

## Growing

Feather reed grass grows best in **full sun**. The soil should be **fertile, moist** and **well drained**. Heavy clay and dry soils are tolerated. Rain and heavy snow may cause it to flop temporarily, but it quickly bounces back. Cut feather reed grass back to 2–4" in very early spring before growth begins. Divide feather reed grass if it begins to die out in the center.

## Tips

Whether it's used as a single, stately focal point, in small groupings or in large drifts, feather reed grass is a desirable, low-maintenance plant. It combines well with perennials that bloom in late summer and fall.

## Recommended

*C.* x *acutiflora* 'Karl Foerster' (Foerster's feather reed grass), the most popular selection, forms a loose mound of green foliage from which the airy, bottlebrush flowers emerge in June. The flowering stems have a loose, arching habit when they first emerge but grow more stiff and upright over summer. Watch for a recent introduction called **'Avalanche,'** which has a white center stripe. Another cultivar is **'Overdam,'** a compact selection with white leaf edges.

*C.* x *acutiflora* 'Overdam' (above)
*C.* x *acutiflora* 'Karl Foerster' (below)

*If you like the way feather reed grass holds its flowers high above its mounded foliage, consider* Deschampsia *(tufted hair grass) and* Molinia *(moor grass) species and cultivars. Some have foliage with creamy yellow stripes.*

**Features:** open habit, becoming upright; silvery pink flowers that turn rich tan; green, possibly white-striped, foliage turns bright gold in fall; winter interest **Height:** 3–5' **Spread:** 2–3' **Hardiness:** zones 4–9

# Fountain Grass
*Pennisetum*

*P. setaceum* 'Rubrum'

Fountain grass's low maintenance and graceful form make it easy to place. It will soften any landscape, even in winter.

## Growing
Fountain grass thrives in **full sun** in **well-drained** soil of **average fertility**. Plants are drought tolerant once established. They may self-seed but are not troublesome. Shear perennials back in early spring and divide them when they start to die out in the center.

## Tips
Fountain grass can be used as individual specimen plants, in group plantings and drifts, or combined with flowering annuals, perennials, shrubs and other ornamental grasses. Annual selections are often planted in containers.

## Recommended
Popular perennials include *P. alope-curoides* 'Hameln' (dwarf perennial fountain grass), a compact cultivar with silvery white plumes and narrow, dark green foliage that turns gold in fall.

Annuals include *P. glaucum* 'Purple Majesty' (purple ornamental millet), which has blackish purple foliage and coarse, bottlebrush flowers. Its form resembles a corn stalk. *P. setaceum* (annual fountain grass) has narrow, green foliage and pinkish purple flowers that mature to gray. 'Burgundy Giant' is a large cultivar with suffused burgundy-purple foliage and pendulous panicles. 'Rubrum' (red or purple annual fountain grass) has broader, deep burgundy foliage and reddish purple flowers.

---

**Features:** arching, fountain-like habit; silvery pink, dusty rose to purplish black foliage; pinkish purple flowers; winter interest **Height:** 2–5' **Spread:** 2–3' **Hardiness:** zones 5–8 or grown as an annual

# Lily-of-the-Valley
*Convallaria*

The dainty bells of lily-of-the-valley possess a heady scent. The flowers are sometimes hidden within the folded leaves, and it isn't until you walk by and detect the sweet perfume wafting past that you think to look for them.

## Growing

Lily-of-the-valley grows well in **partial sun to full shade**. The soil should be of **average fertility**, **humus rich** and **moist**, but almost any soil conditions are tolerated. This plant is drought resistant.

Division is rarely required but can be done whenever you need plants for another area, if flowering is diminished or if you want to share with fellow gardeners. The pairs of leaves grow from small pips, or eyes, that form along the spreading rhizome. Divide a length of root into pieces, leaving at least one pip on each piece.

## Tips

This versatile groundcover can be grown in a variety of locations. It is a good plant to naturalize in woodland gardens, perhaps bordering a pathway or beneath shade trees where little else will grow. It also makes a good groundcover in a shrub border, where its dense growth and fairly shallow roots will keep the weeds down but won't interfere with the shrub's roots.

Lily-of-the-valley can be quite invasive. It is a good idea not to grow it with plants that are less vigorous and likely to be overwhelmed, such as alpine plants in a shady rock garden. Give lily-of-the-valley plenty of space to grow and let it go. Avoid planting it in a place where you may later spend all your time trying to get rid of it.

*C. majalis* var. *rosea* (above), *C. majalis* (below)

## Recommended

***C. majalis*** forms a mat of foliage. Small arching stems lined with fragrant, white, bell-shaped flowers are produced in spring. Many cultivars are available bearing either white or pink nodding blossoms.

**Features:** habit; white, pink flowers; foliage
**Height:** 6–12" **Spread:** indefinite
**Hardiness:** zones 2–7

# Lilyturf
*Liriope*

Often confused with mondo grass (*Ophiopogon* genus), this grass-like perennial is commonly used throughout the state because of its graceful evergreen leaves, showy flowers, clump-forming growth habit and usefulness as a groundcover and edging along borders.

## Growing

Lilyturf prefers **full sun** or **partial shade**. **Light, moderately fertile, moist, well-drained** soil is best.

## Tips

A row of lilyturf planted along a border edge creates a defined, ornate line separating the bed from the lawn or a pathway, sidewalk, patio or driveway.

## Recommended

*L. muscari* is a clump-forming perennial with arching, grass-like foliage. In late summer, flower spikes supporting bright purple flowers emerge from the crown. Cultivars are available with white flowers or variegated silvery or golden foliage. **'Big Blue'** bears violet blue flowers. **'Monroe White'** produces white flower spikes held above dark green foliage. **'Variegata'** produces green leaves with creamy yellow edges and purple flowers.

*L. muscari* (above), *L. muscari* 'Variegata' (below)

*The flowers of lilyturf are followed by small, black, berry-like fruit.*

**Also called:** monkey grass
**Features:** purple, violet blue, white flowers; grass-like foliage in dense clumps
**Height:** 8–24"  **Spread:** 12–24"
**Hardiness:** zones 6–10

# Maiden Grass
*Miscanthus*

M aiden grass is one of the most popular and majestic of all the ornamental grasses. Its graceful foliage dances in the wind and makes an impressive sight all year long.

## Growing
Maiden grass prefers **full sun.** The soil should be of **average fertility, moist** and **well drained,** although some selections tolerate wet soil. All selections tolerate drought once established.

## Tips
Give maiden grass room to spread so you can fully appreciate its beautiful form. This grass creates dramatic impact in groups or as seasonal screens. The height of each selection determines the best place for it in the border.

## Recommended
*M. sinensis* offers numerous cultivars, all distinguished by the white midrib on the leaf blade. Some popular selections include '**Gracillimus**' (maiden grass), with long, fine-textured leaves; '**Grosse Fontaine**' (large fountain maiden grass), a tall, wide-spreading, early-flowering selection; '**Morning Light**' (variegated maiden grass), a short and delicate plant with fine, white leaf edges; **var.** *purpurescens* (flame grass), with foliage that turns bright orange in early fall; and '**Strictus**' (porcupine grass), a tall, stiff, upright selection with unusual horizontal yellow bands.

*M. sinensis* 'Strictus' (above)
*M. sinensis* cultivar (below)

*Maiden grass flowerheads make an interesting addition to fresh or dried flower arrangements.*

**Also called:** eulalia, Japanese silver grass
**Features:** upright, arching habit; colorful summer and fall foliage; pink, copper, silver flowers in late summer and fall; winter interest
**Height:** 4–8'  **Spread:** 2–4'
**Hardiness:** zones 5–9, possibly zone 4

# Painted Fern • Lady Fern
*Athyrium*

A. niponicum var. *pictum* 'Metallicum' (above), A. felix-femina (below)

Lady ferns are some of the most well-behaved ferns, adding color and texture to shady spots without growing rampantly out of control.

### Growing
These ferns grow well in **full shade, partial shade** or **light shade.** The soil should be of **average fertility, humus rich, acidic** and **moist.** Division, rarely required, can be done to propagate more plants.

### Tips
Lady ferns and painted ferns form an attractive mass of foliage but without growing out of control the way some ferns do. Include them in shade gardens and moist woodland gardens.

### Recommended
*A. **felix-femina*** (lady fern) forms a dense clump of lacy fronds. The available cultivars include dwarf ones and plants with variable foliage.

*A. **niponicum** var. **pictum*** 'Metallicum' (Japanese painted fern) forms a clump of dark green fronds with a silvery or reddish metallic sheen. There are many other cultivars with differing colors of foliage available.

*With its metallic shades of silver, burgundy and bronze, the colorful foliage of the Japanese painted fern will brighten up any shaded area.*

**Features:** clumping habit; lacy, sometimes colorful foliage **Height:** 12–24"
**Spread:** 12–24" **Hardiness:** zones 3–9

# Snow-on-the-Mountain

*Aegopodium*

*O*n the right location, snow-on-the-mountain will flourish and fill an otherwise difficult place in no time flat. This invasive plant will fill the space with color, grace and stature and it rarely allows anything to stand in its way.

## Growing

Snow-on-the-mountain grows well in any light conditions from **full sun to full shade**. Soil of **poor fertility** is recommended to curb invasiveness, but any **well-drained** soil is fine. This plant is drought tolerant. Division is rarely required, but you will have to dig up any parts of the plant that are venturing into undesired areas.

If the foliage starts to look bedraggled during summer, you can cut the plants back completely—even mow them down—and they will sprout fresh new growth.

## Tips

Though this groundcover plant can be used almost anywhere, it is best to plant it either where it has lots of room to spread or where its spread can be restricted. Good places include steep banks that are difficult to mow, in the dry shade under a tree where nothing else will grow, in planters or where a natural barrier is created such as the area between a house, walkway and driveway.

Snow-on-the-mountain thrives on neglect. It is an excellent choice for growing at a cottage or other infrequently used property, where there isn't much time to maintain a lawn. Avoid planting this perennial near a lawn, as it

*A. podagraria* 'Variegatum' (above & below)

will quickly creep in. It is an attractive alternative to a lawn under large shade trees where the lack of light and water will be a benefit rather than a detriment to this plant.

## Recommended

*A. podagraria* is rarely grown because it is unstoppably invasive. The cultivar **'Variegatum'** has attractive, white-margined foliage. It is reputed to be less invasive than the species, but it is still very prone to spreading if left unchecked.

**Also called:** bishop's weed
**Features:** variegated foliage, spreading habit
**Height:** 12" **Spread:** indefinite
**Hardiness:** zones 2–8

# Switch Grass
*Panicum*

*P. virgatum* cultivar (above)
*P. virgatum* 'Heavy Metal' (below)

A native to the prairie grasslands, switch grass naturalizes equally well in an informal border or a natural meadow.

### Growing
Switch grass thrives in **full sun, light shade** or **partial shade**. Although the soil should be of **average fertility** and **well drained,** this plant adapts to moist or dry soils and tolerates conditions ranging from heavy clay to lighter, sandy soil. Cut switch grass back to 2–4" from the ground in early spring. The flower stems may break under heavy, wet snow or in exposed, windy sites.

### Tips
Plant switch grass singly in small gardens or in large groups in spacious borders or, for a dramatic, whimsical effect, at the edges of ponds or pools. The seedheads attract birds, and the foliage changes color in fall, so place this plant where you can enjoy both features.

### Recommended
*P. virgatum* (switch grass) is suited to wild meadow gardens. It has a number of popular cultivars. **'Heavy Metal'** (blue switch grass) is an upright plant with narrow, steely blue foliage flushed with gold and burgundy in fall. **'Prairie Sky'** is an arching plant with deep blue foliage. **'Shenandoah'** (red switch grass) has red-tinged, green foliage that turns burgundy in fall.

**Features:** clumping habit; green, blue or burgundy foliage; airy panicles of flowers; fall color; winter interest **Height:** 3–5'
**Spread:** 30–36" **Hardiness:** zones 3–9

# Vinca

*Vinca*

Commonly known as an evergreen groundcover plant, vinca is far more than that. Its reliability is second to none, and its ease of growth is sure to please.

## Growing

Grow vinca in **partial to full shade**. It will grow in **any type of soil** but will turn yellow if the soil is too dry or the sun is too hot. Divide vinca in early spring or mid- to late fall, or whenever it is becoming overgrown. One plant can cover almost any size of area.

## Tips

Vinca is an attractive groundcover in a shrub border, under trees or on a shady bank. It is shallow-rooted and able to out compete weeds but won't interfere with deeper-rooted shrubs. It also prevents soil erosion.

Vinca can be sheared back hard in early spring. The sheared-off ends may have rooted along the stems. These rooted cuttings can be potted and given away as gifts, or they can be introduced to new areas of the garden.

*V. minor* (above & below)

## Recommended

*V. major* is an evergreen, spreading or trailing plant with dark green leaves and blue-purple flowers. **'Variegata'** produces green leaves with white edges.

*V. minor* forms a low, loose mat of trailing stems. Purple or blue flowers are borne in a flush in spring and sporadically throughout summer. This species has smaller leaves than the former. **'Illumination'** produces yellow variegated foliage and bluish flowers.

---

**Also called:** periwinkle, myrtle **Features:** trailing foliage; purple, blue, white, reddish purple mid-spring to fall flowers **Height:** 4–8" **Spread:** indefinite **Hardiness:** zones 4–8

# Wintercreeper
*Euonymus*

*E. fortunei* cultivar (above & below)

Wintercreeper is a hardy, vigorous plant that can be grown as a vine with support, or left to grow without support as a groundcover. Its lush, green summer foliage changes to shades of purple and burgundy in cool days of fall and winter for extended seasonal appeal.

## Growing
Wintercreeper prefers **partial to full shade**. Soil of **average to rich fertility** is preferable, but any **moist, well-drained** soil will do.

*Euonymus translates as 'of good name'— rather ironically named, given that all parts of these plants are poisonous and violently purgative.*

## Tips
Wintercreeper can be grown as a climber with support or as a groundcover if left to trail along the ground.

## Recommended
*E. fortunei* is rarely grown in favor of the wide and attractive variety of cultivars. These can be prostrate, climbing or mounding evergreens, often with attractive, variegated foliage. **'Coloratus'** is an evergreen that spreads moderately fast and can be walked upon. The foliage turns red or purple over winter. It is considered invasive in some areas. **'Kewensis'** is a dwarf selection with white variegated foliage that turns burgundy in fall. **'Wolong Ghost'** is less hardy than 'Coloratus' but also less invasive. It bears elongated, dark green leaves with silver veins.

**Features:** colorful foliage; habit
**Height:** 6–8"  **Spread:** 18" to indefinite
**Hardiness:** zones 5–9

# Glossary

**Acidic soil:** soil with a pH lower than 7.0

**Annual:** a plant that germinates, flowers, sets seed and dies in one growing season

**Alkaline soil:** soil with a pH higher than 7.0

**Basal foliage:** leaves that form from the crown, at the base of the plant

**Bract:** a modified leaf at the base of a flower or flower cluster

**Corm:** a bulb-like, food-storing, underground stem, resembling a bulb without scales

**Crown:** the part of the plant at or just below soil level where the shoots join the roots

**Cultivar:** a cultivated plant variety with one or more distinct differences from the species, e.g., in flower color or disease resistance

**Deadhead:** to remove spent flowers to maintain a neat appearance and encourage a longer blooming season

**Direct sow:** to sow seeds directly in the garden

**Dormancy:** a period of plant inactivity, usually during winter or unfavorable conditions

**Double flower:** a flower with an unusually large number of petals

**Espalier:** a tree trained from a young age to grow on a single plane—often along a wall or fence

**Genus:** a category of biological classification between the species and family levels; the first word in a scientific name indicates the genus

**Grafting:** a type of propagation in which a stem or bud of one plant is joined onto the rootstock of another plant of a closely related species

**Hardy:** capable of surviving unfavorable conditions, such as cold weather or frost, without protection

**Hip:** the fruit of a rose, containing the seeds

**Humus:** decomposed or decomposing organic material in the soil

**Hybrid:** a plant resulting from natural or human-induced cross-breeding between varieties, species or genera

**Neutral soil:** soil with a pH of 7.0

**Offset:** a horizontal branch that forms at the base of a plant and produces new plants from buds at its tips

**Panicle:** a compound flower structure with groups of flowers on short stalks

**Perennial:** a plant that takes three or more years to complete its life cycle

**pH:** a measure of acidity or alkalinity; the soil pH influences availability of nutrients for plants

**Rhizome:** a root-like, food-storing stem that grows horizontally at or just below soil level, from which new shoots may emerge

**Rootball:** the root mass and surrounding soil of a plant

**Seedhead:** dried, inedible fruit that contains seeds; the fruiting stage of the inflorescence

**Self-seeding:** reproducing by means of seeds without human assistance, so that new plants constantly replace those that die

**Semi-double flower:** a flower with petals in two or three rings

**Single flower:** a flower with a single ring of typically four or five petals

**Species:** the fundamental unit of biological classification; the entity from which cultivars and varieties are derived

**Standard:** a shrub or small tree grown with an erect main stem, accomplished either through pruning and training or by grafting the plant onto a tall, straight stock

**Sucker:** a shoot that comes up from the root, often some distance from the plant; it can be separated to form a new plant once it develops its own roots

**Tender:** incapable of surviving the climatic conditions of a given region and requiring protection from frost or cold

**Tuber:** the thick section of a rhizome bearing nodes and buds

**Variegation:** foliage that has more than one color, often patched or striped or bearing leaf margins of a different color

**Variety:** a naturally occurring variant of a species

# Index of Recommended Species Plant Names

Entries in **bold** type indicate the main plant species; *italics* indicate botanical names.

*Acer*, 89
*Achillea*, 67
Adam's needle. *See* Yucca, 68
*Aegopodium*, 167
**Ajuga**, 157
**Allium** (bulb), 137
  drumstick, 137
**Allium** (herb), 148
Althea. *See* Rose-of-Sharon, 103
*Amelanchier*, 105
*Anethum*, 149
Angel wings. *See* Caladium, 138
*Aquilegia*, 44
**Arborvitae**, 69
  eastern, 69
*Artemisia* (herb), 155
*Artemisia* (perennial), 66
Artemisia, silvermound.
  *See* Wormwood, 66
*Asclepias*, 42
**Aster**, 37
  busy, 37
  New England, 37
*Athyrium*, 166

**Bacopa**, 11
**Barberry**, 70
  Japanese, 70
**Basil**, 147
Bean, Egyptian. *See*
  Hyacinth bean, 132
Bean, Indian. *See* Hyacinth
  bean, 132
Bean, lablab. *See* Hyacinth
  bean, 132
**Beautyberry**, 71
  purple, 71
**Beautybush**, 72
**Beebalm**, 38
**Begonia**, 12
  tuberous, 12
  wax, 12
*Berberis*, 70
Bergamot. *See* Beebalm, 38
Bishop's weed. *See* Snow-on-
  the-mountain, 167
**Bittersweet vine**, 127
Bittersweet, American. *See*
  Bittersweet vine, 127
**Black-eyed Susan**, 39

Bluebeard. *See* Blue-mist
  shrub, 40
**Blue-mist shrub**, 40
Boneset. *See* Joe-Pye weed, 56
**Bonica**, 115
Bonica '82. *See* Bonica, 115
Bonica Meidiland. *See*
  Bonica, 115
*Boston ivy*, 135
Buckbrush. *See* Coralberry, 74
*Buddleia*, 41
Bugleweed. *See* Ajuga, 157
Bugleweed, upright. *See*
  Ajuga, 157
**Butterfly bush**, 41
  orange-eye, 41
**Butterfly weed**, 42

**Caladium**, 138
*Calamagrostis*, 161
*Calibrachoa*, 25
**Calla lily**, 139
Calla, golden. *See* Cally lily, 139
Calla, white. *See* Calla lily, 139
Calla, yellow. *See* Calla lily, 139
*Callicarpa*, 71
*Campsis*, 134
**Canna**, 140
*Capsicum*, 26
*Caragana*, 97
*Caryopteris*, 40
**Castor bean**, 13
*Catharanthus*, 35
**Catmint**, 43
Cedar. *See* Arborvitae, 69
Cedar, eastern white. *See*
  Arborvitae, 69
*Celastrus*, 127
*Celosia*, 14
Celosia, crested. *See*
  Cockscomb, 14
Celosia, plume. *See*
  Cockscomb, 14
Celosia, wheat. *See*
  Cockscomb, 14
*Celtis*, 83
*Cercis*, 102
*Chaenomeles*, 101
**Chives**, 148
**Chokecherry**, 73

*Chrysanthemum*, 52
**Cinnamon fern**, 158
Cinquefoil. *See* Potentilla, 99
Cinquefoil, shrubby. *See*
  Potentilla, 99
**Clematis**, 128
**Climbing hydrangea**, 129
**Cockscomb**, 14
**Coleus**, 15
**Columbine**, 44
  Canada, 44
  common, 44
  European, 44
  wild, 44
**Coneflower**, 45
Coneflower, shining. *See*
  Black-eyed Susan, 39
*Convallaria*, 163
**Coral bells**, 46
**Coralberry**, 74
  Chenault, 74
**Coreopsis**, 47
  thread-leaf, 47
*Cornus*, 77
*Corylus*, 80
*Cosmos*, 16
  annual, 16
  chocolate, 16
*Cotinus*, 106
**Cotoneaster**, 75
  cranberry, 75
  rockspray, 75
**Crabapple**, 76
**Crimson Glory**, 116
**Crocus**, 141
  Dutch, 141
  saffron, 141
**Cup flower**, 17
Currant, Indian. *See* Coral-
  berry, 74

**Daffodil**, 142
**Daylily**, 48
**Dead nettle**, 159
  spotted, 159
Demon. *See* Bonica, 115
**Dianthus**, 49
**Dill**, 149
**Dogwood**, 77
  red-twig, 77

yellow-twig, 77
Tatarian, 77
**Don Juan, 117**

*Echinacea,* **45**
Egytian star. *See* Pentas, 28
*Elaeagnus,* **104**
**Elderberry, 78**
black, 78
European, 78
Elephant's ears. *See*
Caladium, 138
**Elm, 79**
Chinese, 79
lacebark, 79
**English ivy, 160**
Eulalia. *See* Maiden grass,
165
*Euonymus,* **170**
*Eupatorium,* **56**
sweet, 56

**Fan flower, 18**
**Feather reed grass, 161**
Foerster's, 161
**Fennel, 150**
bronze, 150
Florence, 150
Fern, flowering. *See*
Cinnamon fern, 158
**Filbert, 80**
contorted, 80
European, 80
Flame grass. *See* Maiden
grass, 165
Fleece vine. *See* Silver-lace
vine, 133
Fleeceflower. *See* Persicaria, 60
Fleeceflower, white. *See*
Persicaria, 60
*Foeniculum,* **150**
**Forsythia, 81**
**Fountain grass, 162**
annual, 162
dwarf perennial, 162
purple annual, 162
red annual, 162
**Fragrant Cloud, 118**
Friesia. *See* Sunsprite, 125
Garlic, round-headed. *See*
Allium, 137
*Gaura,* **65**
**Geranium, 19**
bedding, 19
ivy, 19

scented, 19
zonal, 19
**Gladiolus, 143**
Glory vine, Crimson. *See*
Grape, 130
**Golden-rain tree, 82**
**Goldenrod, 50**
**Grape hyacinth, 144**
Armenian, 144
common, 144
**Grape, 130**
*Gymnocladus,* **87**

**Hackberry, 83**
American, 83
common, 83
Hardhack, golden. *See*
Potentilla, 99
**Hardy hibiscus, 51**
**Hardy mum, 52**
Hazel, corkscrew. *See*
Filbert, 80
Hazelnut. *See* Filbert, 80
Hazelnut, European. *See*
Filbert, 80
Heart-of-Jesus. *See*
Caladium, 138
*Hedera,* **160**
*Helichrysum,* **22**
*Hemerocallis,* **48**
**Hens and chicks, 53**
*Heuchera,* **46**
*Hibiscus* (perennial), **51**
*Hibiscus* (shrub), **103**
**Honeysuckle, 131**
Brown's, 131
coral, 131
goldflame, 131
Japanese, 131
Hall's, 131
scarlet trumpet, 131
trumpet, 131
**Hosta, 54**
**Hyacinth bean, 132**
*Hydrangea* (shrub), **84**
bigleaf, 84
lacecup, 84
mophead, 84
oakleaf, 84
panicle, 84
Peegee, 84
smooth, 84
vine, 84
*Hydrangea,* **129**
*Hypericum,* **109**

**Impatiens, 20**
Busy Lizzie, 20
New Guinea, 20
*Ipomoea,* **27**
**Iris, 55**
Japanese, 55
Siberian, 55
*Itea,* **111**
Ivy, Boston. *See* Virginia
creeper, 135
Ivy, Common. *See* English
ivy, 160

Japanese creeper. *See* Virginia
creeper, 135
**Japanese pagoda, 85**
**Joe-Pye weed, 56**
sweet, 56
Juneberry. *See* Serviceberry, 105
**Juniper, 86**
Chinese, 86
common, 86
creeping, 86
Rocky Mountain, 86
savin, 86
singleseed, 86
*Juniperus,* **86**

**Kentucky coffee tree, 87**
**Knockout, 119**
Knotweed. *See* Persicaria, 60
*Koelreuteria,* **82**
*Kolkwitzia,* **72**

*Lablab,* **132**
Lablab. *See* Hyacinth bean, 132
Lady fern. *See* Painted fern, 166
**Lamb's ear, 57**
Lamb's tails. *See* Lamb's ear, 57
Lamb's tongues. *See* Lamb's
ear, 57
*Lamium,* **159**
*Lantana,* **21**
Leek, lily. *See* Allium, 137
*Leucanthemum,* **64**
**Licorice plant, 22**
*Ligustrum,* **100**
**Lilac, 88**
Chinese, 88
dwarf Korean, 88
Japanese tree, 88
Rouen, 88
Lilac, Summer. *See* Butterfly
bush, 41
*Lilium,* **145**
**Lily, 145**

Lily, white arum. *See* Calla
    lily, 139
**Lily-of-the-valley, 163**
**Lilyturf, 164**
*Liriope*, 164
**Lobelia, 23**
*Lonicera*, 131

*Maclura*, 96
Madagascar periwinkle. *See*
    Vinca, 35
Magilla perilla. *See* Perilla, 29
*Mahonia*, 94
Mahonia, creeping. *See*
    Oregon grape holly, 94
**Maiden grass, 165**
    variegated, 165
    large fountain, 165
*Malus*, 76
**Maple, 89**
    amur, 89
    red, 89
    Shantung, 89
    sugar, 89
    Tatarian, 89
**Marigold, 24**
    African, 24
    American, 24
    Aztec, 24
    French, 24
    signet, 24
    tiploid, 24
Meidomonac. *See* Bonica, 115
*Mentha*, 151
Michaelmas daisy. *See* Aster, 37
Mile-a-minute plant. *See*
    Silver-lace vine, 133
Milkweed, Swamp. *See*
    Butterfly weed, 42
Milkweed. *See* Butterfly
    weed, 42
Millet, purple ornamental.
    *See* Fountain grass, 162
**Million bells, 25**
**Mint, 151**
    orange, 151
*Miscanthus*, 165
**Mock orange, 90**
    virginal, 90
*Monarda*, 38
*Morus*, 91
    white, 91
Moss pinks. *See* Phlox, 61
Moss rose. *See* Rose moss, 32

Mother-in-law plant. *See*
    Caladium, 138
**Mulberry, 91**
*Muscari*, 144
Myrtle. *See* Vinca, 169

*Narcissus*, 142
**Nearly Wild, 120**
*Nepeta*, 43
**New Dawn, 121**
*Nierembergia*, 17
**Ninebark, 92**
    common, 92
Nuage Parfume. *See* Fragrant
    Cloud, 118

**Oak, 93**
    bur, 93
    chinkapin, 93
    English, 93
    Shumard, 93
    Texas, 93
    yellow chestnut, 93
*Ocimum*, 147
Onion, blue globe. *See*
    Allium, 137
Onion, Flowering. *See*
    Allium, 137
Onion, giant. *See* Allium, 137
Onion, golden garlic. *See*
    Allium, 137
**Oregano, 152**
    Greek, 152
    Kaliteri, 152
**Oregon grape holly, 94**
    Oregon, 94
*Origanum*, 152
**Ornamental pear, 95**
**Ornamental pepper, 26**
**Ornamental sweet potato, 27**
**Osage Orange, 96**
*Osmunda*, 158
Oswego tea. *See* Beebalm, 38

*Paeonia*, 58
**Painted fern/Lady fern, 166**
    Japanese, 166
*Panicum*, 168
    blue, 168
    red, 168
*Parthenocissus*, 135
**Pea shrub, 97**
Pear, Callery. *See* Ornamen-
    tal pear, 95
*Pelargonium*, 19

Pelargonium, scented. *See*
    Geranium, 19
*Pennisetum*, 162
**Pentas, 28**
**Peony, 58**
Peppermint. *See* Mint, 151
**Perennial salvia, 59**
**Perilla, 29**
Periwinkle. *See* Vinca, 169
*Perovskia*, 62
**Persian shield, 30**
**Persicaria, 60**
**Petunia, 31**
*Philadelphus*, 90
**Phlox, 61**
    blue, 61
    creeping, 61
    early, 61
    garden, 61
    moss, 61
    woodland, 61
*Physocarpus*, 92
*Picea*, 108
**Pine, 98**
    Austrian, 98
    limber, 98
    Southwestern white, 98
Pink, cheddar. *See* Dianthus, 49
Pink, cottage. *See* Dianthus, 49
Pink, maiden. *See* Dianthus, 49
Pinks. *See* Dianthus, 49
*Pinus*, 98
Plaintain lily. *See* Hosta, 54
Pleurisy root. *See* Butterfly
    weed, 42
*Polygonum*, 133
Porcupine grass. *See* Maiden
    grass, 165
*Portulaca*, 32
**Potentilla, 99**
**Privet, 100**
    Amur, 100
    golden vicary, 100
*Prunus*, 73
Purslane. *See* Rose moss, 32
*Pyrus*, 95

*Quercus*, 93
**Quince, 101**

**Rainbow's End, 122**
**Redbud, 102**
    Eastern, 102
Redcedar, eastern, 86
Red-osier. *See* Dogwood, 77

*Rhus*, 110
*Ricinus*, 13
Rose mallow. *See* Hardy
     hibiscus, 51
**Rose moss, 32**
**Rosemary, 153**
**Rose-of-Sharon, 103**
*Rosmarinus*, 153
*Rudbeckia*, 39
**Russian olive, 104**
**Russian sage, 62**

**Sage, 154**
Sage. *See* Salvia, 33
Sage. *See* Wormwood, 66
Sage, blue. *See* Salvia, 33
Sage, meadow. *See* Perennial
     salvia, 59
Sage, mealy cup. *See* Salvia, 33
Sage, scarlet. *See* Salvia, 33
Sage, silver. *See* Wormwood, 66
Sage, white. *See* Wormwood, 66
**Sally Holmes, 123**
**Salvia, 33**
*Salvia*, 154
*Sambucus*, 78
Saskatoon. *See* Serviceberry, 105
*Scaevola*, 18
**Scentimental, 125**
**Sedum, 63**
     autumn joy, 63
*Sempervivum*, 53
**Serviceberry, 105**
     alder-leaved, 105
     apple, 105
     saskatoon, 105
**Sevillana, 124**
Shadberry. *See* Serviceberry,
     105
**Shasta daisy, 64**
Shiso. *See* Perilla, 29
Silver grass, Japanese. *See*
     Maiden grass, 165
**Silver-lace vine, 133**
Smokebush, purple. *See*
     Smoketree, 106
Smokebush. *See* Smoketree,
     106
**Smoketree, 106**
     American, 106
Snakeroot, white. *See* Joe-Pye
     weed, 56
Snowberry. *See* Coralberry,
     74

Snowberry, common. *See*
     Coralberry, 74
**Snow-on-the-mountain, 167**
*Solidago*, 50
*Sophora*, 85
Spearmint. *See* Mint, 151
**Spirea, 107**
     bridal wreath, 107
     Japanese, 107
     Thunberg, 107
     Vanhoutte, 107
Spirea, Blue. *See* Blue-mist
     shrub, 40
**Spruce, 108**
     Black Hills, 108
St. John's wort. *See* St. Johns-
     wort, 109
**St. Johnswort, 109**
     golden, 109
*Stachys*, 57
Staff vine. *See* Bittersweet
     vine, 127
Star clusters. *See* Pentas, 28
Stars of Persia. *See* Allium, 137
Stonecrop. *See* Sedum, 63
Stonecrop, gold moss. *See*
     Sedum, 63
Stonecrop, showy. *See*
     Sedum, 63
Stonecrop, two-row. *See*
     Sedum, 63
*Strobilanthes*, 30
**Sumac, 110**
     fragrant, 110
     smooth, 110
     staghorn, 110
**Sunsprite, 126**
*Sutera*, 11
Sweet potato vine. *See* Orna-
     mental sweet potato, 27
Sweet William, wild. *See*
     Phlox, 61
**Sweetspire, 111**
**Switch grass, 168**
     red, 168
*Symphoricarpos*, 74
*Syringa*, 88

*Tagetes*, 24
**Tarragon, 155**
*Taxus*, 114
*Thuja*, 69
**Thyme, 156**
     common, 156

     lemon-scented, 156
*Thymus*, 156
Tickseed. *See* Coreopsis, 47
Tickseed, Mouse-eared. *See*
     Coreopsis, 47
Trumpet creeper. *See*
     Trumpet vine, 134
**Trumpet vine, 134**
**Tulip, 146**
*Tulipa*, 146

*Ulmus*, 79

**Verbena, 34**
Verbena, garden. *See*
     Verbena, 34
Verbena, shrub. *See* Lantana, 21
**Viburnum, 112**
     Blackhaw, 112
     Korean spice, 112
     snowball, 112
**Vinca (annual), 35**
**Vinca (groundcover), 169**
**Virginia creeper/Boston
     ivy, 135**
Virgin's Bower. *See* Clematis,
     128
*Vitis*, 130

Walking stick, Harry
     Lauder's. *See* Filbert, 80
**Wandflower, 65**
**Weigela, 113**
**Wintercreeper, 170**
**Wisteria, 136**
     Japanese, 136
Woodbine. *See* Virginia
     Creeper, 135
**Wormwood, 66**

**Yarrow, 67**
     common, 67
Yellow archangel. *See* Dead
     nettle, 159
**Yew, 114**
     English, 114
     English Japanese, 114
     Japanese, 114
**Yucca, 68**

*Zantedeschia*, 139
**Zinnia, 36**
     narrow-leaf, 36

# Author Biographies

**Annie Calovich** is the garden writer for *The Wichita Eagle.* She has a journalism degree from the University of Kansas and has been instructed as a Master Gardener by Kansas State University Research & Extension-Sedgwick County.

**Laura Peters** is a certified Master Gardener with 23 gardening books to her credit. She gained valuable experience in every aspect of the horticultural industry in a career that has spanned more than 18 years. She enjoys sharing her practical knowledge of organic gardening, plant varieties and gardening products with fellow gardeners.

# Acknowledgments

A big thank you to Sedgwick County extension agent Bob Neier for all his help, as well as to Terry Mannell of the Ellis County Extension Service; the Sedgwick County Master Gardeners, especially Charlene Schneider and Norma Kemp; Duane Petersen of Ferns & Foliage in Wichita; Arnold's Greenhouse in LeRoy; and Johnson's Garden Center in Wichita.

*Annie Calovich*

A big thanks to my parents, Gary and Lucy Peters and my friends for their endless encouragement and support all these years. I would also like to thank Annie Calovich for her hard work and her immense knowledge of everything Kansas. Lastly, thanks to all the people who allowed me to photograph their gardens. Without you, this book would have been a lot less fun and colorful. Have fun gardening!

*Laura Peters*